Developing Intimacy with God

An Eight-Week
Prayer Guide
Based on Ignatius'
"Spiritual Exercises"

ALEX B. ARONIS

ISBN: 1-4033-6942-9 (e-book)
ISBN: 1-4033-6943-7 (Paperback)
ISBN: 1-4033-6944-5 (Dust Jacket)

This book is printed on acid free paper.

Illustrations by David MacCoy

All Scripture quotations, unless otherwise indicated, have been taken from the Holy Bible: New International Version®. NIV®. Copyright © 1973, 1978, 1984 by International Bible Society. Used by permission of Zondervan Publishing House. All rights reserved.

The author wishes to thank Loyola Press for granting permission to quote extensively from "*The Spiritual Exercises of St. Ignatius: Based on Studies in the Language of the Autograph*," translated by Louis J. Puhl, S.J. (Chicago: Loyola University Press, 1951).

1stBooks – rev. 04/14/03

I dedicate this book to the individuals who granted me the privilege of guiding them through the devotional prayer program. These fellow Christians are etched in my mind and heart as persons who made prayer a top priority. They spent hours with me in joyful feedback sessions as we talked about their experiences in prayer and as we marveled over the magnificence of Jesus.

CONTENTS

PART I: SEEING YOURSELF AS GOD SEES YOU

PART II: THE LIFE AND MINISTRY OF CHRIST

PART III: THE SUFFERING OF CHRIST 139

PART IV: THE RESURRECTION OF CHRIST 159

ACKNOWLEDGMENTS

Special thanks go to Father John McAnulty, S.J., Director of the House of Prayer for Priests, Los Angeles, California, who introduced me to Ignatius' *Spiritual Exercises.* During the past 20 years, Father McAnulty has met with me on numerous occasions to answer questions and to guide me in Ignatian spirituality. He has helped me grow in my understanding and esteem of Ignatius and the extraordinary contribution he has made to the spiritual life of the Christian church

I am also grateful to a number of persons who read the manuscript and shared their insights and suggestions. I feel a special debt of gratitude to my roommate at the Naval Academy, now a distinguished author and Professor Emeritus of English, Dr. Robert J. Higgs. He provided a continuous flow of suggestions and encouragement throughout the process of writing and rewriting the book. Significant recommendations also came from William Shell, Dennis E. Hensley, Thomas Green, S.J., Lynda Graybeal, Frederick Dale Bruner, John Gilmore, James T. Eilertsen, and George Traub, S.J. Other readers to whom I am grateful are my daughter, Tina Bascom, Blair Cook, Jim Menninger, R. Jackson Painter, Joyce Shumann, Ken Damon, Scott Gruner, Dennis Evans, Georgina Schmits, and Robert Stease.

Warm appreciation is also extended to my good friend and former parishioner, David MacCoy, who provided the artwork for the "With Christ," "Like Christ," "For Christ" illustrations.

Encouraging me to write this book during the past few years has been Karen Navera, a dear friend keenly sensitive to God's will, who has faithfully supported me in intercessory prayer. Helping me with numerous tasks involved in this project was another esteemed friend, my former Administrative Assistant at Kenwood Baptist Church, Shirley Horton. To both, and to many others — especially from Kenwood

Baptist Church and the Union Church of Manila — who have encouraged me and prayed for me, I am indebted.

Most importantly, I express special appreciation and love to my wife, Carol, who made many excellent suggestions for the improvement of this book and who assumed additional family responsibilities so I could devote numerous evenings and weekends to the accomplishment of it. She is the joy of my life.

Through the help of these generous individuals, I am pleased to present the teachings and prayer guidelines contained in this book.

PREFACE

Some years ago I met with a friend on several occasions to talk about prayer. The more we interacted, the more I realized that he knew much more about the subject than I.

Sensing that he was a gentle man, I made myself vulnerable by asking, "John, what do you think I need for spiritual growth?"

He responded without hesitation, "Alex, what you need is a more personal relationship with Jesus."

The words stung. At the time, I was an American Baptist pastor serving as a Navy chaplain. My Sunday sermons regularly urged men and women to receive Jesus so that they could enter into a vital relationship with him. In fact, I had invited Jesus into my life 23 years before because I specifically wanted to know God personally. I had even become a Baptist mainly because that denomination emphasizes a personal relationship with the Lord. Despite all of this, I was being told that what I valued most highly — my relationship with Christ — was somehow deficient.

My pride had been hurt, but even more disturbing and puzzling to me was that this critique came from a Roman Catholic priest. John was Father John McAnulty, S.J. (Society of Jesus), director of the House of Prayer for Priests in Los Angeles, California. And even though I considered John a spiritual man, I found myself wondering (unfairly) "What do Catholics know about a personal relationship with God?"

I had arrived at the House of Prayer for Priests that afternoon feeling spiritually complacent. His comment left me flustered. I wasn't sure I could agree with or trust his assessment.

But in the days that followed, John's words kept coming back to me, and my heart kept telling me that his evaluation was correct. The honeymoon experience of joy that had been mine when I'd first received Jesus into my life had largely faded. I had to admit that I was not experiencing intimacy with God. Also significant to me was the realization that despite the many books I had read, seminars I had attended, and training I had received, I wasn't sure how to revitalize my relationship with Christ nor how to deepen and enrich it.

It took me a couple of weeks before I was ready to call John and ask if he would help me develop a closer relationship with Jesus. He suggested an eight-day retreat in which he would guide me through *The Spiritual Exercises of St. Ignatius*. That retreat, with its focus on praying over the ministry, teachings, suffering, death, and resurrection of Jesus, turned out to be an extremely significant experience. John exposed me to new forms of prayer, helped me become more sensitive to the leadership of the Holy Spirit in prayer, and guided me into a deeper experience of intimacy with Jesus. These were blessings I wanted to share with the Navy men and women whom I served.

I asked Father McAnulty if he would function as my supervisor as I directed five sailors, a sailor's wife, and a chaplain in Ignatius' Exercises. The plan was to stretch the eight-day retreat with five prayer periods each day into eight weeks of prayer training with one prayer period each day. This would serve as my doctor of ministry dissertation project at Fuller Theological Seminary. He agreed, commenting that Ignatius intended his Exercises to be used for persons in various states of life, including those who could not separate themselves from their employment for a private retreat.

When I completed the project 20 years ago, several persons read my dissertation, *Spiritual Direction: A Project Modeled on St. Ignatius' Exercises*,[1] and urged me to write this book. They believed the public would be interested in its teachings. But I did not feel ready. There was too much I still needed to learn.

At the time, I was serving as senior pastor of the Union Church of Manila, an international, interdenominational church in the Philippines. During my five years there, I taught the prayer material, refining and tailoring it for members of our church, for missionaries from a variety of mission organizations, and for seminary students at the Asian Theological Seminary. I always received an enthusiastic response.

From Union Church of Manila, I was called to serve as senior pastor at Kenwood Baptist Church, Cincinnati, Ohio. My 12 years there gave me additional time to develop and refine what I have come to call "Devotional Prayer," which I am now recommending in this book.

There is no shortage of books on prayer, but the books, in and of themselves, seem to do little to improve one's prayer life. Susan Wise Bauer, in her Christianity Today article "The Myth of a Better Prayer Life," laments that "Bagfuls [sic] of books on this subject showed me I wasn't struggling alone."[2] These Christian writings, she concluded, seem almost interchangeable. She found many beneficial explanations regarding prayer, but reading the books made little difference in her prayer life. Bauer concluded by saying that she was searching for a partner in prayer. She was praying for a spiritual director who would be "a wise and mature companion in prayer."[3]

For 20 years, I have served as a spiritual guide to a variety of people largely on a one-on-one basis and have tried to be the kind of partner in prayer that Bauer described: "a wise and mature companion in prayer." Since I cannot personally serve as your guide, I have written this book to assist you in prayer. My book not only explains the types of prayers you will be using and the skills you will need, but, unlike most books on prayer, it coaches you over an eight-week period through a series of interactive prayer exercises. This written guide or curriculum is for individual or group use. It can be used most effectively by meeting once a week with a mentor or spiritual tutor or someone who has gone through the eight weeks of prayer training in this book. However, if such person is not available, the book has been written so that you can proceed on your own, using the book as your personal spiritual guide.

Perhaps your relationship with God has grown distant, even cold, as mine had. Like so many others, you may never have been taught how to experience and nurture intimacy with the Lord. Even though you may be a faithful follower of Jesus — attending church, involving yourself in various religious activities, perhaps even having a consistent "quiet time" — the intimacy of daily communion with Christ is missing. If you see yourself in any of these descriptions and want to deepen your relationship with Christ and experience intimate communion with him, this book is for you.

INTRODUCTION
PREPARING FOR THE JOURNEY

You are about to embark on an eight-week adventure that will significantly deepen your relationship with God. This book introduces you to various methods of prayer and provides step-by-step, interactive prayer exercises. These exercises will increase your love for Christ, broaden your self-understanding, connect you with vital spiritual principles, intensify your desire to become more like Jesus, and strengthen your commitment to serve him by serving others. Your spiritual director will be the Holy Spirit. Gradually, the Spirit will teach you to abide in the Lord's presence, with an awareness of his immediate presence at a deeper level. My role will be to provide instruction, suggestions, and encouragement without getting in the way of the Spirit.

I refer to this total process as Devotional Prayer and consider it among the highest priorities in life. Devotional Prayer enables us to develop intimate knowledge of Christ and as a result increases our desire to keep the commandment which Jesus described as most important: "Love the Lord your God with all your heart and with all your soul and with all your mind and with all your strength" (Mark 12:30).*

SELF-FOCUS TO CHRIST-FOCUS

My experience in directing people in prayer on a one-on-one basis has convinced me that the vast majority of Christians have developed bad habits in their devotional prayer practices. I have found, to an alarming degree, that they focus on their need to improve themselves rather than on God's gracious acceptance of them. Even though they know that they are not saved by their efforts, they have difficulty resting in God's love. Without realizing it, they take on a not-so-subtle "works"

---

* Unless otherwise indicated, all Bible quotations are from the New International Version of the Bible.

mentality, seeking to make themselves more worthy by trying harder. They forget that God does not relate to them on the basis of performance but on the basis of his free gift of grace.

When, for example, they meditate on the Scripture, they zero in on the verses that challenge them to have more integrity, humility, love, and faithfulness. These are diligent Christians who want to be more like Jesus. They are eager to be more powerful in prayer and effective in their service for Christ. And they think they can make these changes in behavior through their efforts, not realizing that they must go through a process of inner transformation. When they fail to see significant improvement in their attitudes and behavior, they become discouraged, imagining that God is as disappointed with them as they are with themselves. Sadly, many of them give up on their "quiet time."

Why do they give up? Because their devotions are not devotional! Their focus is on their deficiencies rather than on the goodness and loving-kindness of God. Consequently, they rarely experience delight in the Lord during their time of prayer. Instead their devotions are often dry and burdensome. These persons desire intimacy with a loving and gracious God, but typically give up in frustration without finding the closeness to God that they seek.

This is not to suggest that as followers of Jesus we can be indifferent to the moral requirements of Scripture. The high moral ground of the Sermon on the Mount and of many other Bible passages lets us know that personal righteousness counts immensely, that God expects us to be diligent in keeping the moral law. But we keep the moral law not to impress God or to prove ourselves worthy. Rather, we obey the commandments of God out of a motive of love. Jesus repeatedly taught that if we love him we will obey what he commanded (John 14:23).

The challenge, therefore, is to increase our love for God. In that way, we will find ourselves growing in our ability to keep the first commandment and also growing in our desire to follow the other teachings of Jesus.

How do we deepen our love for Christ? We do it through a process of inner transformation, primarily by meditating on his life here on earth so that we can understand how "wide and long and high and deep" is

God's love for us (Ephesians 3:17-19). We also do it by remembering that he loved us while we were (and are) still sinners (Romans 5:8; 1 Timothy 1:15). That he loved us first (1 John 4:7-11) means that his love is based on nothing we do. We are loved by God just as we are because that is the nature of love, as God demonstrated in Jesus' sacrificial life and death.

Throughout this book, our task will be to gain a better appreciation of God's extraordinarily great love for us. We will also learn how to experience that love during our time of prayer until his love saturates our whole being. This, I believe, will help us move along the same path taken by the earliest disciples of Jesus.

Taken Up with the Person of Jesus

What fueled the fire of devotion and commitment in the hearts of the disciples? I believe it was their growing awareness and experience of Jesus' compassion, humility, wisdom, and power. The more they witnessed and experienced his goodness and love, the more they wanted to follow him.

Think of the apostles, for instance, terrified by the fury of the wind and the waves on the Sea of Galilee. They woke Jesus up, asleep in the stern of the boat, hoping that he would somehow save them. When Jesus calmed the howling winds and raging waves with a command, the disciples turned to one another in amazement and asked the question they spent the rest of their lives pondering: "What kind of a man is this? Even the winds and the waves obey him!" (Matthew 8:27).

Or consider the foot-washing episode. Jesus knew that within a few hours, his disciples would abandon him; yet with towel and basin he got on his knees to do the task of a household servant. The humble action of Jesus demonstrated unreserved love for the disciples, including even Judas who was about to betray Jesus. This image of servant leadership lodged itself deeply in the minds of the disciples and served as a powerful reminder that they also were to offer themselves as servants to one another.

The disciples spent their days watching Jesus, listening to Jesus, talking about Jesus, imitating Jesus, and ultimately worshiping Jesus.

They had the privilege of being eyewitnesses to his majesty (2 Peter 1:16), and their desire was to know him better and to align their lives with his purposes. Their focus was almost entirely on him, not on themselves.

Resistance to Fixing Our Eyes on Jesus

You would think that Christians would gladly embrace a similar focus. But they do not. Even when I explain the benefits and urge mature men and women of faith to keep their eyes on Jesus, they frequently ignore my counsel unless they are trained through this or some other prayer program. The predictable pattern is to bypass verses that speak of Jesus' compassion and graciousness and instead gravitate to verses in the same passage that reveal deficiencies on the part of the disciples or of other persons in the narrative. Rather than rejoice in the virtues of Christ, they see themselves in the shortcomings of others, pray for forgiveness, and make resolutions to do better.

Let me illustrate. Let's assume that we turn for devotions to the Story of the Prodigal Son (Luke 15:11-32). As we begin reading we may find ourselves identifying with the longings of the younger son. There may still be something of the rebel in us, a repressed yearning to get away from it all, to experience the far country and the raw enjoyments of life that it offers.

As we think about these things we feel some alarm. We call on God to root out the lust and rebellion and unfaithfulness still in us, and to replace it with more dedication, more obedience. We want to be like Christ and so we ask God to forgive us and cleanse us. We conclude with a short prayer for assistance and go forth to be God's man or woman for the day.

The next morning, we go back to the Prodigal Son story. This time, we focus on the elder brother and find ourselves empathizing with him. He had worked hard for the father all those years. It doesn't seem fair that the younger brother, the prodigal, should be treated like a star. And as we think about our relationship to God, we have to admit that, like the older son, we sometimes feel left out and resentful.

But we don't want to accuse God, so we confess our lukewarm faith and our self-righteous tendencies, and ask God to make us kinder, more compassionate, more like Christ. We conclude with a brief prayer and move out hoping we can be Christ's person in the workplace.

Notice what has happened. We have had two devotions that were not really devotions. They were exercises in self-examination and character development. What we did was to identify with the faults of the younger son on the first day and with the faults of the older son on the second day. On the third day we probably would have turned to another passage of Scripture to search for some principle of living that we were neglecting, some commandment that we were disobeying, or some sin that we were concealing.

We fall into this rut again and again. It's almost as though we enjoy saying to ourselves, "I am not cutting it." "I am falling short." "I am not like Jesus." "I must do better." And, of course, the "accuser of the brethren" (Revelation 12:10) is having a wonderful time telling us how wretched we are as Christian disciples. After we admit our weaknesses and make resolutions for improvement, we go forth to sin again.

What should we do? Take our eyes off of self and fix our eyes on Christ. That is the only way to devotion. Let's remind ourselves of the meaning of that descriptive word. To be devoted is to be ardently dedicated to a person, loyal to a person, in love with a person. How do we intensify our dedication to, love for, and delight in Christ? By noticing how great he is, looking for qualities that we can admire, observing the many reasons he is worthy to be our Lord.

The main point of the story is not the younger son's careless dissipation or the older son's angry resentment. There's nothing new or significant in the sins of these brothers. What is new and remarkable is the incredible kindness and goodness of the Father. He spotted his son in the distance, ran to embrace him, interrupted his apology, restored him into the family, and threw a party to celebrate his return from death to life. Then he went after the older son. The Father reasoned with him, pleaded with him, assured him that everything he had was also his. And what Jesus wanted his listeners to realize and appreciate was that he, himself, was relating to them — and that he relates to us — in precisely the same manner as the Father related to the two sons: with patience, understanding, forgiveness, generosity, and love.

As we meditate on this classic story, as we ponder God's love and acceptance of us, the Holy Spirit may give us a gift of joy or tears. We will want to stay with that joy and adore God, or with those tears and cry for a while. The objective of devotions is not simply to read a Bible story or even to meditate on it, but to experience intimacy with the Father, with Jesus, with the Spirit. And as we delight in the Lord, our devotion is deepened. We go forth with gladness to serve the God who meets with us and loves us in spite of our weaknesses.

How long does it take to learn to have devotions that are truly devotional? Three to five weeks. It takes that long for people to become persuaded that the fastest way to compassion and graciousness in their lives is to delight in Christ's compassion and grace. Personal transformation takes place as a result of noticing in increasing depths how wonderful Jesus is. The author of Hebrews makes the point cogently: "Let us fix our eyes on Jesus, the author and perfecter of our faith" (Hebrews 12:2).

A Christian Revolution

Throughout this book I will encourage you, even implore you, to focus on the qualities you see in Jesus rather than dwell on the deficiencies you see in yourself. I will urge you to become more sensitive to the truth Christ always expressed rather than fret over the untruths you sometimes express. I will ask you to notice Christ's grace always present in his interactions with others rather than fuss over the anger occasionally present in your interactions. I will do this not because our sins are unimportant, but because transformation happens when we "fix" our eyes on Jesus, not on our many faults.

"The great Christian revolutions," said H. Richard Niebuhr, "come not by the discovery of something that was not known before. They happen when somebody takes radically something that was always there."[1] My desire in this book is to help us take radically the opportunity to do something that has been possible all along but has been neglected by many. I want us to shift our prayer concentration from ourselves to a prayer concentration that delights in the grace and truth of Jesus, abides in him with heightened sensitivity, and results in a life that seeks only to know, love, and serve him.

I often wonder why it takes so long to shift from a self-focus to a Christ-focus. Perhaps the resistance can be traced to the self-centeredness deeply ingrained in each of us, the desire for self-justification activated by our pride, and the deceit of the enemy of our souls whose denunciations turn our eyes away from Jesus and on to ourselves.

"WITH CHRIST, LIKE CHRIST, FOR CHRIST!"

As we turn to the Scriptures on the life and ministry of Jesus during the next eight weeks, most of the prayer exercises will have the following objective: "Intimate knowledge of Christ that I might be *with* him, become *like* him, and live *for* him." These three prepositions *with* — *like* — *for* help maintain perspective. They express the essential sequence of steps necessary for the transformation of our souls.

Notice the progression in the three-fold sequence. First is time *with* Christ; next is growth in becoming *like* Christ; and last is service offered *for* Christ. The three steps are interrelated and mutually supportive. However, communion *with* Christ takes the lead. The apostles began, and we ourselves must begin, by being *with* Christ: "He appointed twelve, that they might be *with* Him" (Mark 3:14, italics added).

The sketches shown below remind us of this sequence and of the necessity of beginning *with* Christ. (The bold print in the verses has been added for emphasis.)

7

"With Christ"
"He appointed twelve ...
that they might be **with** *Him."*
Mark 3:14

"Like Christ"
"And we, who ... contemplate
the Lord's glory, are being
transformed into his **likeness**
with ever increasing glory."
2 Corinthians 3:18

"For Christ"
"He died for all, that those
who live should no longer live
for themselves but **for** *him*
who died for them and was
raised again."
2 Corinthians 5:14-15

"With Christ"

It is customary for pastors to urge their congregations to spend time with Christ in prayer. They know that this is of paramount importance, that it is the better choice, the one thing needful, as Jesus, himself, said (Luke 10:42). But the exhortations to pray and the instructions given by the pastors usually have to do with praying for others or praying for personal needs. Rarely does one hear instruction on how, specifically, one can increase devotion and adoration for God, how one can nurture and deepen one's relationship with Jesus.

The approach that I have taken begins by inviting the Holy Spirit to help us gain intimate knowledge of Christ that we might love him more. The Spirit responds by directing our attention to the grace and wisdom of Jesus. This is what Jesus said the Holy Spirit would do: bring glory to Jesus and teach us all that belongs to him (John 16:14-15). We meditate on these qualities of Jesus using a variety of prayers explained in this eight-week prayer guide. These methods of prayer enable the person praying to become more sensitive to the leadership of the Holy Spirit.

When the Holy Spirit guides us in prayer, we are actually *with* Christ since the Spirit is the Spirit of Christ (2 Corinthians 3:17-18). We are also *with* Christ as we adore him, offer prayers of petition and intercession to him, and imaginatively place ourselves in the story to gain intimate knowledge of him.

At the conclusion of the prayer period, I encourage individuals to enter into a prayer of rest. This involves a shift from rational reflection to an inward stillness that enables us to abide in peaceful fellowship with Christ. It is our privilege to commune *with* Jesus at this deeper, more intimate level. By faith, we can affirm that the Lord Jesus lives within. It is a reality that Jesus emphasized (John 14:20, 17:23, 17:26); a mystery that reveals the hope of a believer's glory (Colossians 1:27); and a promise that disciples are to claim – "Never will I leave you; never will I forsake you!" (Hebrews 13:5).

In his autobiography *Just as I Am*, Billy Graham described the many ways God used him during his nearly 60 years of ministry. But toward the end of his book he expressed regret that he had not spent more time communing with the Lord. If he had to do it all over again he said he would "spend more time in spiritual nurture, seeking to grow closer to God so that I could become more like Christ."[2] He went on to say that he would also spend more time meditating on the Bible.

Bill Bright, founder of Campus Crusade for Christ and considered by many as being responsible for introducing more people to Christ than anyone else, gave a similar answer when asked, "In hindsight would you have done anything differently?" Bright at 78 years of age said, "If I had to live my life over, I would have concentrated on getting to know God better and love him more and trust him more."[3]

When I consider the expressions of regret from these two giants of Christian leadership, Billy Graham and Bill Bright, I wonder how much more dynamic their ministries might have been if they had given greater concentration to being *with* Christ and becoming *like* Christ instead of focusing so much of their time and effort on service *for* Christ. The good news is that we don't have to feel sorrow in the twilight years of our lives for not spending more time getting closer to God. Most of us can make the decision much earlier to engage in regular, intimate communion *with* Christ.

"Like Christ"

Communing regularly *with* Christ through Devotional Prayer transforms us inwardly so that we increasingly become *like* him in character, motivation, assumptions, values, goals, and behavior. Paul describes this process in 2 Corinthians 3:18: "And we all, with unveiled face, beholding the glory of the Lord, are being changed into his likeness from one degree of glory to another" (RSV).

This important passage of Scripture describes us as "beholding" (RSV) the glory of the Lord. Some translations use the verb "contemplate" (NIV) rather than behold. As we behold or contemplate his glory, the verse indicates that we are "changed" (RSV) or "transformed" (NIV) into his likeness.

Some have suggested that Paul had Moses in mind when he wrote this passage, for Moses came down from Mount Sinai with his face aglow reflecting the glory of the Lord (Exodus 34:29-30). Paul may also have had Jesus in mind when his face shone like the sun and his clothes

10

became as white as the light on the Mount of Transfiguration. The verb used to describe what happened to Jesus in the Gospels of Matthew (17:2) and Mark (9:2) is "transfigured" (*metamorphoo*), and this is the same verb Paul uses to indicate that we are "changed" (RSV) (*metamorphoo*) or "transformed" (NIV) (*metamorphoo*) into his likeness.

Moreover, Paul says, "we are being changed into his likeness from one degree of glory to another" (RSV) or that "we are being transformed into his likeness with ever-increasing glory" (NIV). The tense that Paul uses in "are being transformed" is the present continuous tense. John Stott, the British evangelical theologian and author, pointed out that "the glory of Jesus Christ which we behold, and into which we are being changed, does not fade like the glory on the face of Moses, or even like the glory of the temporarily transfigured Jesus. On the contrary, it increases from one degree to the next."[4]

That is not to say that we reach perfection in this life. As Paul indicates, we are "being changed" into Christ's likeness. Those words tell us that there is plenty of room for growth. Along this line, Stott observed that "the Christian life is a progressive 'metamorphosis' into Christ's image, a steady, ongoing, unceasing process of becoming more *like* him" (italics added).[5]

In Devotional Prayer, we behold the Lord's glory by seeking it out, meditating on it, adoring Christ for it, and resting in it. And while we are beholding the glory of the Lord and communing with him, the Holy Spirit does his inward, sanctifying work (2 Corinthians 3:18). He adjusts our thoughts and intentions by giving us a passion to have Christ's own character within our lives. We devote ourselves to becoming more and more like Jesus. In this way, the Spirit transforms us and enables us to make progress, in small increments, on the second aspiration of the prayer exercise objective: "become *like* him."

"For Christ"

"*With* Christ!" "*Like* Christ!" "*For* Christ!" The three form a progression in which each is connected to the other. The first deals with devotion, the second with character, the third with service. Those who spend time in the company of Christ are increasingly shaped into his likeness and will want to offer themselves in service *for* Christ.

The problem is that our concentration is almost exclusively on service *for* Christ. When, for example, a pastor meets a new church member, he often thinks in terms of discovering, developing, and deploying this person's spiritual gifts. The intention is not to teach this person to be *with* Christ or to become *like* Christ, but to engage him or her in service *for* Christ. This is often the case because the church needs ushers, or additional members for committees or boards, or for the choir, or Sunday school teachers and helpers, or hostesses for small groups. After a few years of service *for* Christ, the enthusiasm of the new member often fades and he or she often drops out feeling tired and used.

Nationally known author, pastor, and radio Bible teacher Charles Swindoll took a break from the demands of the pastorate and was able to look with new eyes at the ministry in general and the church in particular. In his journal he recorded that his appraisal led him to a growing concern over the busyness of so many in the churches. He noted that this heavy involvement in the church left them feeling weary, resentful, and empty. One clergyman whispered to him, "I'm operating on fumes. I am lonely, hollow, shallow, enslaved to a schedule that never lets up."[6] As Swindoll embraced him, the man wept with deep, heaving sobs.

This led to more serious thinking and reading and praying until Pastor Swindoll arrived at the heart of what seemed to him to be the core issue. He expressed it this way:

> *A lack of intimacy. Pure and simple. That best defines
> the problem. An absence of intimacy with the Almighty.
> Involvements, yes, but not intimacy. Activities and
> programs aplenty, but not intimacy* (italics added).[7]

The teaching and exercises in this book are designed to show us how to experience intimacy *with* Christ. Intimacy provides the medium through which the Holy Spirit makes us more *like* Christ, and inspires us to give ourselves in service *for* Christ.

"The Spiritual Exercises of St. Ignatius"

The principles and methods of prayer I teach in this book are based on Scripture and the insights that have come to me from my studies in

Reformed and evangelical theology. However, as I indicated in the Preface, I have also benefited significantly in my understanding of prayer by working with Ignatius' *Spiritual Exercises*.

Ignatius of Loyola (1491-1556)[8] was a sixteenth-century Roman Catholic Christian who organized a series of methods and activities for opening oneself to God's Spirit and allowing one's whole being, not just the mind, to be affected. Ignatius had a deep love for Christ and wanted those he guided in prayer to "smell the infinite fragrance, and taste the infinite sweetness of the divinity."[9] In 1541 Ignatius' handbook was completed and came to be called *The Spiritual Exercises of St. Ignatius*. It has been among the treasured writings on spirituality for more than 450 years and has provided extremely valuable assistance to those who seek to be disciples of Jesus.[10]

Dallas Willard, in his insightful book *The Divine Conspiracy*, wrote that *The Spiritual Exercises of Saint Ignatius* is among the most profound treatments of discipleship to Jesus. He said that if one makes the necessary adjustments to the content of such a work, one will see that it offers, in substance, "a curriculum, a course of training,"[11] for life as a disciple of Jesus.

The necessary adjustments to the content of Ignatius' *Spiritual Exercises* that Willard recommends are what I have attempted. To the uninitiated, Ignatius' *Spiritual Exercises* is difficult to grasp since it was not written as a self-help manual but as a compilation of notes mainly for those who guide others in prayer. Its usefulness is further complicated because the *Exercises* reflect sixteenth-century terminology, images, and theology. My adaptation of the *Exercises* attempts to maximize its contributions for modern readers.

Organization of the Eight-Week Prayer Guide

The Prayer Guide in this book is divided into four major parts similar to Ignatius' four-fold division in his *Spiritual Exercises*.

Part I: "Seeing Yourself as God Sees You"

Part I focuses on foundational principles and on God's love despite any shortcomings we may have. The meditations in Part I will give us a sense of where we are spiritually as we begin this prayer journey.

13

Part II: **"The Life and Ministry of Christ"**

Part II deals with the life and ministry of our Lord. It gives us intimate knowledge of Jesus. It is the heart of the prayer program.

Part III: **"The Suffering of Christ"**

Part III strengthens our commitment to Christ by helping us see that Jesus loves us so much that he suffered and died for us.

Part IV: **"The Resurrection of Christ"**

Part IV enables us to enter into the joy of our resurrected Lord. He empowers us to serve him as our living and glorious Savior and God.

The number of days that a person should spend in each part depends on the needs of the person doing the exercises and the judgment of the person guiding the exercises. I have used an estimate of the time most people stay in each part and have structured Parts I, III, and IV to last one week, and Part II to last five weeks.

Each of my Weeks is made up of three sections: first, instruction on some aspect of Devotional Prayer; second, interactive "Prayer Exercises"; third, a "Friends on the Journey" section. The first section introduces principles and skills needed for the interactive prayer exercises for that week and should be read prior to doing the prayer exercises. The prayer exercises in the second section are to be done normally one day at a time. This can vary, however, with an individual's schedule. A person could do two or more exercises in one day if he separates the sessions by a few hours. The final section, "Friends on the Journey," invites the reader to "sit in" on my interaction with Bob and Cathy, both fictional persons, yet representative of many people who have gone through the prayer program. These two persons raise questions and concerns typically brought up by those who have gone through the prayer exercises.

Letting God love you

As you begin this prayer program, it will be helpful to ask the Lord to increase the intensity of your desire for God. We have different backgrounds, abilities, and time availability. Yet, through the use of the material in this book, the Spirit, if we have the intensity of desire, will lead each of us to greater intimacy with God as we learn to commune with Christ through Devotional Prayer.

Please do not think that the training you will receive in Devotional Prayer will in any way compete or interfere with your public worship of God. On the contrary, as you get closer to Christ in devotional prayer, your ability to commune with the Lord in public worship will improve. Correspondingly, an active involvement in the public worship of God provides an essential balance to the private, personal devotions encouraged by this book.

Also, it may reassure you to know that this training does not require you to have much experience or knowledge about prayer. Prayer is verbal and non-verbal interaction with God. He is pleased when you desire to get close, make requests, listen, and let him love you.

Award-winning author Philip Yancey was waiting in O'Hare Airport for a flight that was delayed for five hours. He had been working on a book that had left him feeling burdened by other people's pains, doubts, and unanswered prayers. A woman who was traveling to the same destination listened to him in silence for a very long time, then asked a question that Yancey says has always stayed with him: "Philip, do you ever just let God love you?" She added, "It's pretty important, I think."[12]

That question caused Yancey to realize "with a start" that she had "brought to light a gaping hole" in his spiritual life. For all of his "absorption in the Christian faith," he wrote, he had "missed the most important message of all."[13]

For disciples of Jesus, nothing in this world is of greater importance than intimacy with Christ. It is our greatest joy and privilege to know Jesus personally, and to let God love us as we commune with him on a daily basis. This eight-week guide in Devotional Prayer will teach you how to do that.

PART I

Seeing Yourself as God Sees You

Part I provides principles of spiritual direction and a series of prayer exercises that invite us to see ourselves as God sees us and to accept ourselves on the basis of God's love for us. The exercises help us to understand and respect the way in which God has been working in our lives. They also help us see some of the ways in which we have resisted and continue to resist God, and to face ourselves on the basis of what God says about us. We enhance this process if we earnestly desire self-knowledge, a true understanding of ourselves.

WEEK 1

WORKING WITH SPIRITUAL DIRECTION

Week One introduces seven basic principles of spiritual direction that are fundamental to the instruction provided in this book. Following the presentation of the principles is a discussion of seven practicalities of prayer that deal with elementary questions of procedure, such as time and place of prayer, prayer postures, and centering approaches. These particulars may seem obvious, but attention to simple details can make a significant difference.

SEVEN PRINCIPLES OF SPIRITUAL DIRECTION

1.   Understand that God welcomes you just as you are.

During this prayer program, we will open our hearts to God to the extent that we believe he desires our companionship. Some of us will come to God eagerly, as to a Friend we know and love. Others of us may be reluctant to approach God because we are afraid of him or because we hold resentments against him.

Despite any hesitation we might have, we need to be assured that God welcomes each of us as we are. God loves us and has taken steps to establish and sustain a loving relationship with us. Not only has he surrounded us with the beauty of his universe, he has sent his Son, Jesus, to live and die and rise again that we might have new life by believing in him. God is our faithful Lord and Friend. He is always moving toward us to help us, forgive us, and embrace us.

If you feel that you are not worthy to pray to God, be encouraged by the words of the great reformer Martin Luther (1483-1546). He wrote,

> Though I am sinful and unworthy, still I have the commandment of God, telling me to pray, and His promise that He will graciously hear me, not on account of my worthiness, but on account of the Lord Jesus.[1]

Through the centuries, the teachers of the church have helped us realize how great a privilege it is for us to be invited by Jesus to call God "Our Father." Fourth-century patriarch of Constantinople, John Chrysostom (c.345-407), renowned for his courage and eloquence as a preacher, saw in the words "Our Father" a reminder of all of God's bounty. He wrote,

> For he who calls God Father, by him both remission of sins, and taking away of punishment, and righteousness, and sanctification, and redemption, and adoption, and inheritance, and brotherhood with the Only-begotten, and the supply of the Spirit, are acknowledged in this single title. For one cannot call God Father, without having attained to all of these blessings.[2]

2. Recognize that the Holy Spirit is your Spiritual Director.

Jesus said that the Holy Spirit would teach us all things (John 14:26). He does that as we meditate on the Scriptures and pause to listen to his voice. At times, it comes to us as a still, small voice and at other times as a firm, confident voice; sometimes as an impression or an elucidation that results in an inner glow.

Karl Rahner (1904-1984), a prominent theologian, wrote that the human director or "master of the exercises" as he called him, "provides, if he can, quite cautiously and from a distance, an opportunity for *God and man to meet together truly and directly*" (italics added).[3]

This perspective is in line with one of Ignatius' basic tenets. Ignatius believed that a person will experience greater spiritual benefit when he discovers something on his own or from the Spirit enlightening his mind rather than from having someone else interpret God's will or develop the meaning of a Scripture passage for him.[4] That is the reason why I provide only limited commentary on the Bible passages used in the prayer exercises.

3. Seek to be flexible.

Prayer involves delicate, personal interaction between your soul and the Holy Spirit. Rules and precepts cannot orchestrate this sacred intercourse with God. Rather it can occur only as you seek to be flexible and sensitive to the movement of the Spirit during your prayer exercises.

The various prayer modes and skills you will be learning will enable you to shift back and forth interchangeably from one prayer mode to another, and from one insight to another, adapting and moving with freedom as you seek intimate knowledge of Christ. I will remind you of this principle of flexibility often, urging you to ask for the guidance of the Holy Spirit as you seek insight that reveals the greatness of Jesus or that provides self-understanding, or that moves you into a deeper experience of communion with God.

4. Learn to be guided through peace or turbulence.

How do you learn to be attuned to the movement of the Holy Spirit during the prayer exercise? By becoming sensitive to the experience of peace or the lack of it as you pray through a passage of Scripture. Before, during, and after you read the passage, you should be monitoring the inward experience of peace, since it is a primary means by which the Lord guides you. "Let the peace of Christ rule in your hearts" (Colossians 3:15).

As you meditate on a Bible passage and invite the Spirit to communicate insight, you will learn to linger over those words, phrases, thoughts, and images that bring a special sense of peace or seem to be highlighted by the Spirit. At times the passage may provoke within you a disturbance or unrest, a lack of peace. That also needs to be explored by asking the Spirit to reveal the reason behind the disturbance. If there is a need to confess sin and repent, this becomes an important part of the painful but liberating process of self-knowledge.

5. Seek an intimate understanding of the truth.

In the spiritual life, it is better to be impressed deeply with one insight, like finding one precious pearl, than to be more lightly affected by two or three. The savoring of what one has received is a concept which Ignatius emphasized: "It is not much knowledge that fills and

21

satisfies the soul, but *the intimate understanding and relish of the truth*" (italics added).[5] "What is important," according to John J. English, a Jesuit commentator on Ignatius' art of spiritual direction, "is not to get through a great deal of subject matter in prayer but to *grasp profoundly* whatever one prays about" (italics added).[6] Dietrich Bonhoeffer [1906-1945], a highly regarded Lutheran theologian, urged a similar focus in personal meditation, confining oneself to one text, possibly for an entire week.[7]

6. Discern what works for you.

As the prayer session ends, you will be asked to take a few minutes to assess the prayer time. Your goal will be to be utterly simple in discerning the value of any activity in prayer. You will typically ask yourself what you found to be helpful in achieving the objective of your prayer exercise, and what you discovered to be a distraction or hindrance. You will benefit in subsequent prayer exercises by practicing what worked and eliminating what did not.

7. Discuss your prayer experiences with your pastor or spiritual mentor.

If the ideas presented here are new to you, do not hesitate to approach your pastor or spiritual mentor with questions or concerns. If he or she is unavailable, talk with someone with wisdom, experience, and biblical awareness whose spiritual maturity and wisdom you trust.

SEVEN PRACTICALITIES OF PRAYER

Before we turn to the prayer exercises, let's look at some of the practical considerations involved in prayer.

1. Time Involvement

During the first few weeks, each prayer exercise should last approximately 30 minutes and increase as quickly as seems appropriate to a maximum of 60 minutes, not counting the time taken for the review/assessment period. You will probably find yourself moving up to 45 to 60 minutes of prayer time within the first three weeks.

In addition, you will need to read carefully the instruction that precedes the exercises. These remarks will provide background information, introduce skills, and recommend practices that will help you work through the exercises more effectively. If you are scheduled for a work project that takes you away from your residence for several weeks, it would be better to postpone this training until your calendar is clear for an eight-week stretch. The training in this program is cumulative and more beneficial when practice can take place as additional skills are introduced and instructions are provided.

2. Place of Prayer

Select a place of prayer that works best for you. It may be a private room or study, a church or chapel, a picnic table or grass knoll on a bluff overlooking the ocean, a quiet neighborhood or lakeside recreation area in which to stroll. The main requirement for an appropriate place is that it has a minimum of interruptions or distractions, recognizing that what constitutes a distraction will vary with individuals.

Some of the best or worst prayer experiences can be the consequence of location. A telephone that keeps ringing, a couple arguing in the next apartment, a stack of correspondence on your desk next to the Bible you are trying to read and pray over — these and other distractions can wreck efforts to commune with God.

Martin Luther agrees. He writes, "It is a good idea for a person to be alone when he intends to pray, so that he can pour out his prayer to God in a free and uninhibited manner, using words and gestures that he could not use if he were in human company."[8]

3. Time of Day

For many, the early hours are preferred. Morning prayer sets the tone for the rest of the day. But if you are not a morning person, meet

God when you are at your best. For some that will be the noon hour or late afternoon or evening. Others prefer devotions just before sleep. Your work and travel requirements, daily schedule, and availability of space all play a part in your decision as to when to have prayer.

Richard Foster, author of excellent books on spirituality, described an appealing prayer routine you may want to try:

> One winter I scheduled a three o'clock appointment into my date book for each working day. I would then leave the office for one hour, drive five minutes to the local zoo, and, with Bible and personal journal in hand, spend fifty minutes on a bench in a lovely indoor rain forest.[9]

4. Relaxation and Rest

During the prayer program, it is important to keep doing the things that keep you relaxed and connected with your friends and family. Take time to find out how things are going with the neighbors. Ride around the block on a bicycle with the kids. Write a farewell note to a colleague who is retiring. Have heartfelt laughter with high school buddies as you go over the old stories one more time. These are the kinds of experiences that keep us emotionally and socially balanced as we take on the training required by this prayer program.

Also, make sure you are getting enough sleep during the eight weeks of this program. Mental fatigue and physical weariness hinder your ability to pray in a concentrated manner; they are obstacles to spiritual receptivity. If you are feeling exhausted, it would be beneficial to get two or three days of extra rest before you begin the prayer exercises in Week 1.

5. Posture in Prayer

There are a variety of prayer postures. Determine which is best for you through experience. The characteristic options are as follows:

Kneeling: This ancient posture of humility and reverence can be a definite aid in preparing one's spirit for communion with the Lord. I commend it, particularly at the beginning of a prayer period. It has its disadvantages, however, if used for extended time. C. S. Lewis (1893-

1963) pointed out that it is better to sit and concentrate than to kneel and be half asleep.[10]

Sitting: You can pray seated in a chair or at a desk. In meditating on Scripture, it often helps to have a pencil in hand and a pad of paper nearby to record insights. When you shift from meditation to resting quietly in the Lord, move to a more comfortable place like a lounge chair or recliner.

Strolling: A slow walk with Scripture in hand, pausing to meditate on a Bible passage as you stroll through a lovely garden, alongside a lake, or on a beach, may turn out to be very beneficial. Others may find the visual stimulation of an outdoor scene to be a distraction.

Variety of positions: Ignatius' preference was to use a variety of postures:

> I will enter upon the meditation, now kneeling, now prostrate upon the ground, now lying face upwards, now seated, now standing, always being intent on seeking what I desire. Hence ... if I find what I desire while kneeling, I will not seek to change my position; if prostrate, I will observe the same direction, etc.[11]

6. Centering Approaches

We often come to prayer with distracting thoughts competing for our attention. Many people find it helpful to take a few moments to gather their thoughts in the following ways:

Psalms: Christians through the centuries have centered themselves by reading a Psalm or two, especially those written in praise of the Lord as in Psalms 96, 98, 100, 103, 107, 136, 145, 148, 149, 150. Also helpful are Psalms that promote trust in the Lord like Psalms 11, 16, 20, 23, 27, 31, 34, 42, 61, 62, 91, 121. Experiment with these and other Psalms to determine which are most helpful in preparing you for prayer.

Hymns and spiritual songs: To help me gather my thoughts and center on the Lord, I often begin my devotions using the Psalms for one month and then hymns for the next. I find it helpful to sing softly and slowly, being careful to gauge the extent to which a hymn or spiritual song is stirring devotion within. If one hymn is not moving me devotionally, I turn to another. When I find one that stirs me, I stay with it and savor the words or thoughts, allowing myself to be involved in the emotions I feel, singing joyously of God's goodness or sorrowfully over

Christ's wounds. I find this to be a meaningful way to prepare myself for devotional prayer.

Devotional booklets: I advise against devotional booklets during these eight weeks because the booklet meditation will most likely be on a subject different from the one you will be asked to consider during your hour of prayer. It is more helpful to seek the understanding of one truth, as expressed in the fifth principle of spiritual direction, than to mix meditations or themes.

7. Journaling

Keep a diary of your prayer exercises in which you can record insights gained, emotions felt, or words imparted by the Lord. The extent to which you experienced quiet intimacy with Christ should be noted, along with anything unusual during the prayer exercise that enhanced your time in prayer.

Thomas Green, spiritual director of San Jose Seminary in Manila, is an excellent teacher of prayer who emphasizes the journaling of feelings we experience in prayer. As an example, one of Green's entries reads:

> Lord, this hour was very difficult. I found myself distracted and restless, unable to center on you. But I tried to persevere, and in the last moment or two I felt your peace and your reassurance that the time was not wasted.[12]

A major advantage of a journal is that it lets us see the peaks and the valleys of our prayer journey as part of a total experience. When we struggle with dryness in prayer, the journal helps us maintain perspective by reminding us of experiences in prayer when we were coasting with joy. We tend to forget the wonderful consolations God has given us in the past, especially when we find ourselves frustrated by two or three sessions in prayer where God seems absent and our prayers feel empty.

SEVEN PRAYER EXERCISES

In the Introduction, I discussed at length the need to concentrate on Christ rather than self. It may therefore surprise you that during this first week of exercises I will ask you to focus on yourself rather than Christ.

That's because I would like you to have a bench mark of where you are spiritually before you begin the prayer meditations on the life of Jesus. The exercises in Week 1 get you in touch with your deepest aspirations, gifts, hidden sins, and strengths so that you will have a better self-understanding as you begin this prayer program.

You need not come up with final answers to the questions asked in the Week 1 exercises. You will most likely want to change your responses over the eight weeks as you grow in your understanding of God's will for your life. My suggestion is that you see this first week as the start of a bike ride. Get on the bike, and begin to peddle. Later in the prayer training, you will have opportunities to review, confirm, or modify your responses. Don't get stuck or discouraged if you are not fully satisfied with your responses, especially your responses to the first two exercises. Keep moving through the first week. The exercises are preparing you for the prayer course as a whole by helping you see yourself as you really are.

The first exercise, "Basic Want," asks what you are seeking at the core of your being. *"Motivating Statement"* invites you to consider some thought or phrase that will motivate you toward achieving that Basic Want. *"Gifts"* seeks to make you aware of the gifts God has given you and what you would consider to be the best use of those gifts. *"Freedom"* provides an opportunity for you to consider the degree to which you have freedom for God and his will. *"Self-examination"* is an invitation to see yourself in light of the Sermon on the Mount and to find forgiveness in those areas where you may be falling short. *"Solace"* helps you understand how loving and compassionate the Father is toward you. *"Repeat"* permits you to go back to the exercise that was most meaningful for you and to spend an additional half-hour or hour of prayer on it.

Each of the exercises has an "Objective" and is followed by a few accompanying comments or questions to clarify it. A specific Scripture passage is also provided followed by recommendations for "Your Response."

During these first weeks, I suggest that you advance a paragraph at a time through the "Your Response" recommendations. The process will be like learning to skate. After a few weeks, you will be able to relax and, like a competent skater, enjoy the experience without thinking about the mechanics. In four or five weeks, I will make fewer response recommendations so that, by the time you complete eight weeks, you will know what works best for you and will be able to proceed on your own.

Day One: "Basic Want"

<u>Objective</u>:   Determine what you want at the core of your being. (Examples of Basic Want: "Love," "Fully Devoted to God," "Eternal Life," "With Christ, Like Christ, For Christ," "Love, Joy, and Peace," "Intimacy with God," "Servant of God," "To Praise, Reverence, and Serve God," "The Glory of God," "Lead Others to Truth," "To Contribute to the Great Commission Each Day," "Worship," "Fulfill the Great Commandment," "Undivided Dedication to Christ," "Live the Sermon on the Mount," "Peacemaker," "Glorify and Enjoy God," "My Best for His Glory.")

<u>Questions</u>:   Select one of the following questions to concentrate on. What do I consider to be the goal of my life? What would it mean for me to do something really significant? When it's all over, what do I hope I will have accomplished? What do I want for my epitaph? These questions deal with how you view your purpose in life. You are free to make changes or adjustments to your statement of "Basic Want" at any time during your eight weeks of training or thereafter.

<u>Scripture</u>: Psalm 139.

Your Response:

- ✤ Ask the Lord for a strong desire to increase your self-understanding. Also request that he assist you in determining what you want at the core of your being. Example: "Dear Lord, give me a deep desire to know myself better and to see myself as you see me. Open my mind and my heart to focus on the issue of my 'Basic Want.' Grant me your wisdom and enable me to be guided by your Spirit as I consider Psalm 139 and the question of what I am looking for in my life."

- ✤ Select one of the items under the "Questions" section for Day One. Consider it prayerfully and record your answer. Realize that when you pursue an inquiry under the guidance of the Holy Spirit, asking questions and seeking to be sensitive to impressions the Spirit gives, you are interacting with God, communicating with him, and therefore engaging in prayer.

✣ Read through Psalm 139 slowly and thoughtfully. Look for ways in which that passage may help you determine what you want at the core of your being. You may come up with an answer that differs from the one you recorded earlier. Feel free to modify your response according to the light that you receive. Turn to any other Scripture passage that may seem helpful in reaching the objective of the prayer exercise, such as Philippians 3:7-14, John 15:1-17, Psalm 73, or Isaiah 55.

✣ Compare your responses and try to discern which "Basic Want" is most important for you. You need not feel that this will be your final response. Many like to return to this exercise throughout the prayer program and beyond.

✣ Talk to the Lord about your "Basic Want" and ask him to confirm it, modify it, or provide an alternative response consistent with further insight that he may give you either now or later.

✣ Take a few moments to thank the Lord for guiding you in this exercise. Then sit in his presence for a few moments. Instruction on how to do this is provided in subsequent weeks. For now, simply sit quietly and rest in the Lord's presence since he loves you and Christ lives in you. (Galatians 2:20; 2 Corinthians 13:5).

✣ Conclude by thanking the Lord for any increase in self-understanding that he has given you. Also thank him for the privilege of being in his presence. Ask him to fulfill the "Basic Want" of your life.

✣ Review your prayer exercise and consider how you succeeded. If poorly, seek the cause. If well, give thanks, and follow the same method next time. The review at the conclusion of each prayer period normally takes only a few minutes.

Day Two: *"Motivating Statement"*

<u>Objective</u>: Decide on a word, phrase, or statement that best motivates you toward the fulfillment of your "Basic Want."

<u>Question</u>: What phrase, statement, or image can I use to guide me in the direction that I want my life to take? (Examples: "The goodness and loving kindness of God," "Jesus," "Abide," "Beneath are the everlasting arms," "Behold The God-Man," "With Christ, Like Christ, For Christ.") Feel free to make adjustments or to change your "Motivating Statement" at any time during this eight-week program or thereafter.

<u>Scriptures</u>: 1 John 3:16-24; 4:7-21.

Your Response:

- ❖ Ask the Lord to increase your desire for self-understanding and to assist you in finding a "Motivating Statement."

- ❖ Consider the examples of motivating words or phrases above and others that come to mind and list those most appealing to you.

- ❖ Read through the following Bible passages: 1 John 3:16-24; 4:7-21. Use any other Scripture passage that may seem helpful in reaching the objective of the prayer exercise. Add to your list motivational words, phrases, or statements that seem promising. Prayerfully compare words, phrases, and images, then decide on the "Motivating Statement" that influences you most strongly toward the fulfillment of your "Basic Want."

- ❖ Ask the Lord to confirm or modify the "Motivating Statement" that you came up with or to provide something else according to further insight that he may give you at the present time or in the future.

- ❖ Take a few moments to commune with the Lord by sitting quietly before him. Seek to be conscious of his love for you by resting in the assurance given in 1 John 4:8b-10. Also, find comfort in his promise that he is always with you (Matthew 28:20b).

✛ Conclude by asking God to remind you of your "Motivating Statement" and to help you use it regularly to move you toward the fulfillment of your "Basic Want."

✛ Review your prayer period and consider how you succeeded or where you may have hindered the prayer process. Learn to repeat the good things you did and to avoid those things that were counterproductive.

Day Three: "Gifts"

<u>Objective</u>: Give thanks to God for the gifts and blessings in your life and recognize that they have been given to enable you to fulfill your "Basic Want."

<u>Scriptures</u>: Psalm 103; Genesis 1–2; Mark 12:13-17; Romans 12:1-2; 1 Corinthians 10:31.

<u>First point</u>: Give thanks to God for the gifts and blessings God has given to you.

<u>Second point</u>: Seek to understand the relationship between the gifts or blessings and your "Basic Want."

Your Response:

✛ Ask the Lord to assist you in considering, delighting in, and praising him for the gifts and blessings he has given you. Ask also that you be given understanding of the relationship between these gifts and the ways they might be used to fulfill your "Basic Want."

✛ Begin by recalling the blessings and gifts that God has given you as an individual and as a member of the human family. Read Psalm 103 to help you count your blessings. Pause to meditate on this great psalm. Turn to other passages of the Bible that might help you fulfill the objective of the exercise. Genesis 1–2 is a helpful passage in considering gifts God has given to humanity in general and to you as an individual. As you read, delight and give thanks and praise to God for blessings and gifts.

❖ Next, consider how you have used the gifts God has given you and the extent to which you have used them to fulfill your "Basic Want." Suggested Scriptures are Mark 12:13-17; Romans 12:1-2; 1 Corinthians 10:31. If you feel sadness over the misuse of the gifts God has given you, take time to talk this over with the Lord. Confess your neglect and ask for his forgiveness. Ask the Spirit to help you appropriate the promises of grace contained in Psalm 103:11-13. Ask the Lord to increase your desire for the proper use of gifts.

❖ In addition to the gifts you recognized within you and all around you, be grateful for positive emotions you felt as you identified God's gifts to you or for sorrow you felt over the misuse of your gifts. These emotions are also gifts of God that facilitate your interaction with him in prayer.

❖ Take a few moments to thank the Lord for any increase in self-understanding you have received. Then, rest in the Lord's presence and let him love you. Recognize that, despite your weaknesses, he is pleased to be in your company. As Psalm 103:4 indicates, "He crowns you with his love and compassion."

❖ Review your prayer exercise to consider what went well and what did not.

Day Four: "Freedom"

<u>Objective</u>: Desire freedom in relation to everything except God. This is freedom *for* God and for the power he gives to do his will.

<u>Considerations</u>: All things are good for their purposes, but they can be misused. Freedom means that you are liberated from dependence on and obligations to false gods that drive you toward an ever-increasing appetite for greed, praise, and power. Consider whether it may sometimes be better to prefer a simplified lifestyle to a luxurious lifestyle, dishonor over honor, and a short life over a long life.

<u>Scriptures</u>: Luke 16:19-31; Philippians 2:3-11.

Your Response:

✣ Begin by asking the Lord to help you increase your desire for freedom in relation to everything except God. Pray also that the Lord will help you understand some of the attachments in your life that keep you from spiritual freedom.

✣ Read Luke 16:19-31 and meditate on its message as it relates to riches and poverty. Do the same with Philippians 2:3-11 and consider what light it sheds on the issues of a short life versus a long life and dishonor versus honor. If you desire, look at additional Scriptures that touch on these subjects such as James 2:1-13; 5:1-16.

✣ Ask the Lord for an increase in self-understanding as you think about the extent to which you may have an unhealthy attachment to any of the values mentioned in the paragraph above titled "Considerations." Pray that the Lord will give you greater spiritual freedom in relation to everything except himself.

✣ Reflect on whether it would be beneficial from the standpoint of freedom to develop an attitude of neutrality or detachment toward all of the values mentioned in "Considerations." That would mean that if it would serve to honor God, you would be as willing, for instance, to live in luxury as to live in simplicity, or to live in simplicity as to live in luxury.

✣ Take a few moments to abide in his presence, believing in your heart that God loves you very much. Conclude by thanking God for the gift of his presence.

✣ Review your prayer period.

Day Five: "Self-examination"

Objective: Increase in self-understanding that, through the grace of God, I might see myself as God sees me and seek to overcome my sinful tendencies.

Scriptures: Genesis 3; Matthew 5–7; 1 John 1:8-9.

<u>First point</u>: Seek an increase in self-understanding as you consider the story of the fall of humankind (Genesis 3).

<u>Second point</u>: Seek to see yourself as God sees you, as you reflect on the Sermon on the Mount (Matthew 5–7).

<u>Third point</u>: Receive God's forgiveness and love as you move to confession through the consideration of 1 John 1:8-9.

Your Response:

❖   Ask for the Lord's help in achieving the objective of this prayer exercise.

❖   First point: In considering Genesis 3, relate it to the history of humankind, the world today, your own experience.

❖   Second point: Read a part or all of Matthew 5–7. Consider how Jesus announces that we are "salt" and "light." He instructs us in Matthew 5 to reconcile ourselves to others, practice sexual purity and marital faithfulness, preserve integrity in speech, and exercise magnanimity and love for enemies. He commands us in Matthew 6 to impress God, not others; and to trust in God, not materialism. He tells us in Matthew 7 to avoid judging others, to ask for God's help, and to practice the "Golden Rule."

     As you meditate on these passages, remember that God reveals to us our sinful tendencies so that he can reform our lives. He does this by bringing us under conviction, leading us to repentance, forgiving us, giving us a sense of freedom and joy along with sadness, and giving us the courage and strength to change.

     Do not make the mistake of attacking yourself for your weaknesses or failings. That is not helpful. Seek conviction without condemnation. Godly sorrow is good, but not feelings of worthlessness, or obsessive thoughts about sin. God loves us in spite of our sin.

❖   Third point: Carefully consider 1 John 1:8-9. Confess your sins to God. Agree with God's verdict on your sinful behavior and resolve to turn from it and, if appropriate, to make restitution for it. (An example of restitution would be to return stolen property to its rightful owner, extending your apologies and accepting the consequences for your prior action.)

✢ Receive the forgiveness God promises in 1 John 1:8-9. As you do, rest in the love and peace that God provides. Express your gratitude and love to the Lord for the positive and negative things revealed to you during this meditation.

✢ Rest in the Lord's presence for a few minutes, grateful for the increase in self-understanding he is giving you and thankful for forming you more and more into his likeness. Conclude your time of prayer by offering yourself to the Lord.

Day Six: "Solace"

Objective: Express gratitude and praise to God as you achieve deeper understanding of his love and forgiveness.

Scripture: Luke 15:11-32.

First point: The attitude, behavior, and decisions of the younger son.

Second point: The father's response to the younger son.

Third point: The attitude, behavior, and decisions of the older son and the father's response to him.

Your Response:

✢ Begin by asking God for help to attain the objective of the exercise.

✢ Use your imagination as you meditate on this story verse by verse. Apply your five senses to enter into it, reliving it mentally and emotionally. For example watch the younger son ask for his inheritance, listen to the music as he parties with his friends, smell the hog pen where he works, feel the tears run down the father's cheeks as he embraces the son, hear the father shout to his servants, taste the fatted calf.

✢ Be aware of any positive emotions you are feeling, such as sorrow, sadness, compassion, delight, praise, and affection. Pause and linger with those feelings as long as they last by resisting the urge to forge ahead. If the feelings are drawing you closer to the Lord, take time to adore him; then, as the feelings subside, give thanks to him for the consolations. They are his gifts to you.

✣ Deepen your understanding of God's love for you by imaginatively placing yourself in the story as either the younger son and/or the older son. Go through the story one more time personalizing the dialogue as much as you can.

✣ As you achieve a deeper understanding of God's forgiveness and love for you, express your gratitude to him and offer yourself to him.

✣ Humbly and gratefully rest in the Lord's presence for a few minutes. Conclude by thanking God for the opportunity to experience his presence.

✣ Assess your prayer exercise by considering what was helpful.

Day Seven: "Repeat"

Use this *"Repeat"* prayer exercise to return to the exercise that was most helpful to you, or that seemed promising but that you had to cut short, or that you missed.

Some wonder about repeating prayer exercises that were not satisfying or fulfilling the first time through. Their hope is that the prayer period will go better on the second try. Rather than doing this, I suggest that you repeat those sessions where the Holy Spirit ministered to you most deeply. The likelihood is that the Spirit will reveal even more the second or third time through. "Whoever has will be given more, and he will have an abundance" (Matthew 13:12; Mark 4:25).

FRIENDS ON THE JOURNEY

Bob — Prayer and study. a good mix?

Bob traveled regularly during the week and sometimes on weekends. When he got home, he caught up on administrative tasks and spent time with his wife and their three young children.

With so much going on, Bob was neglecting his relationship with God and felt the need for closer communion with Jesus. He asked if I would work with him in the area of Devotional Prayer. I was pleased to meet with him because of his maturity in the faith, teachable spirit, and deep commitment to evangelism. Bob was typical of many engaged in evangelistic work: thoroughly coached in praying for others (intercessory prayer), but minimally trained in Devotional Prayer.

After he concluded the first week of exercises, Bob told me that he had spent a good bit of his time reading Bible commentaries during the time he was supposed to be praying. The commentaries provided him with helpful ideas, but he wondered whether he should have been reading the comments of scholars instead of praying through the assigned Scriptures.

I affirmed the value of study, but suggested he refer to his commentaries or read the notes in his Study Bible the evening before his time in prayer. This would give him an opportunity to reflect on new information before meditating on the passage the following morning. I did not want him to miss the exhilaration that comes when the Holy Spirit himself sheds light on the passage's meaning.

In addition, I pointed out the difference between study and meditation. I explained that study involves the analysis and explanation of a passage, whereas meditation involves an encounter with God's Word in our hearts so that we can ponder it and experience life in God's presence.

Cathy — Dealing with distractions

Cathy came to me in a state of discouragement. She had lost her position in a merchandising firm bought out by a competitor. She needed confidence and an understanding of how God was dealing with her.

I wondered whether her preoccupation with the loss of her employment would prevent her from hearing the still small voice of the Spirit during prayer. I suggested that our time together might be more profitable if we were to wait until she had regained emotional and career stability. But she had great desire to proceed, and I have come to believe that desire is the most important prerequisite for engaging in this prayer program.

During her first week, Cathy was frustrated by distractions during the prayer exercises. As soon as she sat down to pray, there seemed to be a dozen obligations that came to her mind, some very trivial: the dishes needed to be placed in the dishwasher, her cocker spaniel needed to be fed even though she described the dog as "totally low maintenance." In disgust, Cathy complained: "My mind was shouting that the dog needed her dinner right at the time I sat down for devotions." I suggested that she keep a pad of paper handy to write down the obligations that popped into her mind so that she could stop thinking about them until after her prayer time.

Even more discouraging to her was her tendency to put off prayer until it was time to go to bed. She asked if I would hold her accountable at our next meeting by asking whether she had allowed sufficient time each day for her devotions. I agreed, but suggested that she aim for some progress and not be overly concerned if she did not succeed perfectly.

PART II

The Life and Ministry of Christ

The Prayer Exercises in Part II deal with the life and ministry of Jesus. They are the heart of this prayer program since they put us in touch with the extraordinary qualities of Jesus, enabling us to adore him for who he is and for the extravagant gift of his love for us. Part II also provides instruction on various methods of prayer, four types of insights, the Prayer of Rest, dealing with dryness, and making a choice in accordance with God's will.

The training in Weeks 2 through 6 will deepen our knowledge of the grace and truth that emanated from Jesus, increase our freedom to become more like him, and enable us to experience the immediate presence of Christ as we commune with him in prayer.

WEEK 2
PRAYING IN VARIOUS WAYS

We seek intimate knowledge of Christ as we pray over the Gospels. We are helped in doing this by using various methods of prayer. You will learn about these modes of prayer in this chapter and will be coached in their use, not only during this week but also during Weeks 3 through 6. By the end of the prayer program, you will have a clear grasp of how to use each mode of prayer and which to use as you meditate on various passages in the Bible.

METHODS OF PRAYER

Devotional Prayer involves the use of the various prayer methods described below. We use these styles or modes of prayer to call upon the Lord for his help, meditate on the Scriptures, experience God's consolations as gifts, lift our praise and thanksgiving to the Lord, petition him for our needs, adore him for his goodness, and silently abide in his presence. *Ignatius* taught or employed these styles or modes of prayer in various sections of *The Spiritual Exercises*.[1]

Preparatory Prayer

You will be asked to begin each prayer exercise with Preparatory Prayer. Here's an example of this type of prayer: "Dear Father, I have come to have fellowship with you. Increase my desire to know Jesus intimately. Please speak to me through your word and enable me to grow in my love for you. I am grateful that you will be guiding me during this time of prayer. I come to you in Jesus' name. Amen."

In Preparatory Prayer, we approach the God who loves and receives us just as we are, and ask, audibly or inaudibly, for his assistance before every prayer exercise. In this form of prayer, we communicate conversationally with God, speaking as one friend speaks to another.

I strongly encourage you to make a habit of using Preparatory Prayer before each prayer exercise. Pausing to ask for God's assistance demonstrates a humble dependence upon the Lord and reminds us that we are not in control, that we really do need God's grace in order to hear from him, to meet with him, and to receive the blessings he grants during the prayer period.

Mental Prayer

Mental Prayer involves praying over passages of Scripture by engaging one's cognitive and imaginative faculties. There are three sub-categories of Mental Prayer: Meditative Reading, Imaginative Contemplation, and Prayer of Consideration. Initially, we will work with them one at a time so that we can learn the skills involved in each. Later we will be able to shift back and forth, sensing which is most useful for the Bible passage under consideration.

Meditative Reading

From early Christian centuries Meditative Reading has been called *lectio divina*. This Latin phrase, pronounced **lex**-ee-oh di-**vee**-nuh, is translated "divine reading" or "sacred reading."

Meditative Reading involves reading a Bible passage slowly, considering a verse, sentence, or phrase at a time, listening at ever deeper levels for the word God has for us. We will want to read the passage repetitively, preferably out loud, enabling us to interact with the Bible with both our eyes and ears. Ignatius advised that a person meditate upon a word as long as he found "various meanings, comparisons, relish, and consolation in the consideration of it."[2]

In Meditative Reading we realize that God's word for us may take time to emerge. We engage in this form of prayer in much the same way as an antique collector would enter a shop known for its rare treasures. Imagine him or her moving through the room with total concentration, desiring to be aware of the historical significance and the aesthetic appeal of each antique. Just so, in Meditative Reading we sift through the thoughts and words of a passage attentively, seeking to sense their impact upon us. With each repetition, something totally new may come to our attention. When that happens, we weigh the significance of that which impresses us, staying with the emotions called forth and experiencing them as fully as possible.

Sometimes we feel as though we are a part of the events in the narrative and speak to God freely about our concerns or requests. At other times the reading may be dull and prayer may be an effort, but then through patient sifting a special insight breaks through.

Imaginative Contemplation

In Imaginative Contemplation, we use our imagination to visualize the scene, reproducing it in our mind's eye as though watching a film of the event. At times we place ourselves in the scene as an onlooker or as a participant in the action, allowing the drama of the story to make its impact upon us.

In this way of prayer, we use our five senses to enter into the narrative. Thus, in the story of the prodigal son that we meditated on last week, we may have "seen" the father running eagerly to greet the son and "felt" the bearded face of the son next to his father's cheek. We may have "heard" the father interrupt the apology of his son to shout to the servants for the best robe, the ring, the sandals, and the preparation of the fatted calf. Or, we may have "heard" the joyful music and the celebration of neighbors. All of this is in accord with the advice of Ignatius, who urged that we "smell the infinite fragrance, and taste the infinite sweetness of the divinity."[3]

Visualization is a form of prayer that involves right-brain activity. Some people are able to imagine a Bible story clearly (even in Technicolor). Recognize that you have this capability to some extent. You use it every time you remember an event out of your past or every time you wince when someone tells you about hitting his thumb with a hammer. At first you may only be able to imagine bits and pieces of a Bible story. Work with Imaginative Contemplation as best you can. Your ability to visualize will improve with practice.

My caution is that you avoid imagining anything that violates the Bible's moral code or that contradicts Scripture in any way. Reject as quickly as you can any scene that intrudes itself into your mind but that you know is not of the Holy Spirit.

Prayer of Consideration

The Prayer of Consideration involves an analytical approach to the Scripture passage. It aggressively searches for insights in much the same manner as inductive Bible study aggressively analyzes a passage. Both ask the questions: Who? What? When? Where? How? and Why? These questions help us understand and organize the content of the passage. Because the Prayer of Consideration is largely analytical, it is decidedly a left-brain activity.

The difference between the Prayer of Consideration and inductive Bible study is that inductive Bible study is knowledge-oriented, whereas the Prayer of Consideration is prayer-oriented. In the former, we study a passage and gather information to satisfy our curiosity or to teach others. In the latter, we analyze a passage so that we can pray over it. In both, we intentionally bring ourselves under the supervision of the Holy Spirit, asking for his assistance. But in the Prayer of Consideration, we make a point of thanking the Lord as he reveals insights to us, petitioning him for discernment in evaluating the insights, and praising and thanking him for his gifts of consolation provided during the time of prayer.

Heart Prayer

Heart Prayer involves emotions aroused by God's Spirit. The classic example of this prayer is found in the Gospel narrative where the disciples met the resurrected Jesus on the Emmaus road and afterward said, "Were not our hearts burning within us while he talked with us on the road and opened the Scriptures to us?" (Luke 24:32). Divine-human communication was occurring between the Word of Jesus and the emotional response in the hearts of the disciples.

When we read the accounts of Jesus' passion we may sometimes find ourselves moved to a deep sense of sorrow, even tears. Though unspoken, our sense of sorrow and grief is most likely a tender communication of our love for him. And because it is a form of nonverbal communication with God, it is prayer.

Or, as we pray we may occasionally find ourselves gripped by strong emotions that move us to joyful shouts or enthusiastic singing. Since it is the Holy Spirit who sometimes moves us in these ways, we will want to stay with these feelings as long as they continue to well up within us. After the feelings subside and several days have gone by, we can test the source of these feelings by asking whether the experience has increased our love for Christ and others. If we love Christ and others more, we can assume that these emotions were not from the evil one but from the Spirit.

Most church people do not know what to do with their emotions, even when emotions are aroused by the Scriptures, hymns, or spiritual songs. Men, especially, feel embarrassed at becoming emotional. But emotions are very important and give us entry into Heart Prayer, also called "affective prayer." This form of prayer deepens our relationship with God.

John A. Mackay (1889-1983), the late president of Princeton Theological Seminary, once said:

> One of the most important problems the church of today faces is that it regards it lawful to express feelings in every field but religion. What the present church needs is to provide something which will inflame all the human passions.[4]

An overwhelming sense of joy, peace, and excitement may come upon us as the Spirit speaks to us through Scripture. These and other emotions are God's gifts. We must train ourselves to recognize them as such. If we think our emotions are only natural responses that we can produce at will or mere sentimentalism over which we ought to feel shame, we miss the opportunity to discern and appreciate God's gracious work in our hearts. How much better to identify these emotions as God's tender gifts from above, stay with them as long as they last, and thank him for the important part they play in increasing our devotion to him.

Ignatius refers to these gifts as "consolations" and describes them as follows:

> I call it consolation when an interior movement is aroused in the soul, by which it is inflamed with love of its Creator and Lord .... It is likewise consolation when one sheds tears that move to the love of God, whether it be because of sorrow for sins, or because of the sufferings of Christ our Lord, or for any other reason that is immediately directed to the praise and service of God. Finally, I call consolation every increase of faith, hope and love, and all interior joy that invites and attracts to what is heavenly

and to the salvation of one's soul by filling it with peace and quiet in its Creator and Lord.[5]

Prayer of Petition

The Prayer of Petition is the most common type of prayer. It is requesting things from God, as Martin Luther indicated: "To pray ... is to call upon God in every need."[6] French theologian and reformer John Calvin (1509-1564) said that our merciful Father trains us to "seek, ask, and entreat him to our great good."[7] To "request," "entreat," "ask for," or "wish for" our Father's assistance is to use words all of which in Hebrew or Greek are generally translated into the English words "prayer" or "pray for."

The Preparatory Prayer we use at the beginning of each prayer exercise is a prayer of petition because we are asking the Lord to give us spiritual illumination. The Prayer of Petition differs from intercessory prayer in that the latter is offered not for ourselves but for the needs of others.

Some think that asking for our personal needs is a less desirable form of prayer because it seems selfish. But the Lord, Himself, instructed us to ask when he gave us the Lord's Prayer. The seven prayer considerations in the Lord's Prayer are petitions, with four of them so personal that they include the terms "our" and "us." Richard Foster explains that the Prayer of Petition remains primary throughout our lives "because we are forever dependent upon God. It is something that we never really 'get beyond,' nor should we even want to."[8]

During the prayer exercises, you may be prompted to ask, as John Calvin recommends, that your heart be fired with a zealous and burning desire to seek, love, and serve God. Or request that you receive God's benefits with a grateful heart. Or ask that you be led to meditate upon his kindness more faithfully and ardently.[9] At times the petition will be exactly the request you feel God wants you to make, and you will want to record it so that you can keep track of how the Lord answers your prayer.

Prayer of Adoration

In the Prayer of Adoration, we lift our hearts to praise God for who he is in the majesty of his being. We also thank him for what he has done out of his great love for us. There are times when we simply want to shout, "Thank you, God, for who you are and thank you, also, for the extravagant gift of your love!"

Prayers of Adoration can burst forth at any time during our prayer exercise. Our hearts can be set aglow at the beginning, in the middle, or at the conclusion of our prayer period. This happens as God grants us the gift of consolation. We respond by voicing our praise, thanksgiving, and adoration.

But the Prayer of Adoration can also occur quietly toward the end of our prayer period. At that time, we may want to express adoration for the consolations experienced and the knowledge of Christ savored. Our praise for his majesty and power, our love in response to his love, our thanks for his forgiveness and strength are offered in quiet reverence.

Prayer of Rest

I will be suggesting that you conclude most of your prayer exercises with the Prayer of Rest. In this prayer, we move to the immediate experience of God at a deeper, more intimate level. We shift from praise or petition to the realm of silence. We repose in the presence of the Lord without words or images. Our desire is to release all distractions, to surrender to his presence, to bask in God's love, to rest in him in accordance with Jesus' invitation: "Come to me, all you who are weary and burdened, and I will give you rest" (Matthew 11:28).

This intimacy in silence has been described in terms of two lovers on a hilltop with a beautiful valley below. Their love for one another and enjoyment of one another make words unnecessary. Communication is there, but it is a communion beyond words. Each senses the other person's presence, joy, and love in the midst of a beautiful setting. Just so, we rest in the Lord, feeling a deep sense of gratitude that the Ruler of Heaven should condescend to visit us in our humble place of prayer. After we have expressed our adoration and thanks, there is no further need for words.

During the Prayer of Rest, distractions inevitably come. We respond by setting them aside gently without becoming upset with ourselves. We can refocus our minds by going back to the Prayer of Adoration and offer praise once again for the character qualities of Jesus that impressed us. We may then return to the Prayer of Rest. In Week 4, I provide substantially more comment and instruction on this type of prayer.

Infused Prayer

Infused Prayer can take several forms. It can come upon us so that we find ourselves held or affected as by a strong compelling attraction, like a magnificent sunset. Or we can experience the presence of Christ with our faculties quiet but not asleep, as though our ordinary sense faculties were mildly suspended as in the experience of "resting in the Spirit." Again, we can be given a profound sense of union with the will of God. It is not a form of prayer that we enter into of our own volition.

According to John McAnulty, Infused Prayer is "without sufficient previous cause and beyond our normal capacities."[10] It comes upon us when life's circumstances or situations or our emotional moods and dispositions cannot reasonably be expected to contribute to our experience of this prayer. For example, if we are facing a major operation for cancer and have no visitor to cheer us, no written communication or music to encourage us, no other positive influences to lift us, the Lord may nevertheless inspire us with an experience of exquisite joy or profound peace. "Beyond normal capacities" means that we cannot produce such an experience by our own resolve or by fulfilling special conditions.

How does Infused Prayer differ from Heart Prayer? It is a matter of degree. Both Heart Prayer and Infused Prayer are gifts from God and cannot be programmed, but Infused Prayer is a deeper experience of God's grace. Infused Prayer is a more total gift.

Ignatius does not specifically refer to Infused Prayer. However, the following experience of prayer as described by Ignatius is what I would call Infused Prayer. "If in contemplation, say on 'Our Father,' he [the person praying] finds in one or two words abundant matter for thought and much relish and consolation, he should not be anxious to go on, though the whole hour be taken up with what he has found."[11] To find much delight in one or two words through the whole hour is beyond normal capacities. It is a communication that is beyond what circumstances would cause or what one would be able to attain without a special infusion of God's grace.

SEVEN PRAYER EXERCISES

The "Prayer Exercises" during this second week and for the next four weeks will be almost entirely on the life and ministry of Jesus. The first prayer exercise in Week 2 provides a delightful opportunity to leaf through the Gospel of Mark to come up with the scene or episode in the life of Christ that presents him in a way that is most inspiring to you. It is called *"Most Appealing."*[12] The second exercise invites meditation on Jesus as the eternal Word and is titled, *"The Word Became Flesh."* Next are prayer exercises on the *"Annunciation and Visitation," "Jesus' Birth,"* and *"The Boy Jesus at the Temple."* You will also have a prayer exercise that I call *"Repeat."* It invites you to repeat any of the meditations in Weeks 1 or 2. A seventh prayer exercise, called *"Review,"* follows. It allows you to consider whether there might be a common thread in the messages the Lord has been communicating to you during Week 2.

Day One: "Most Appealing"

Objective: Determine what episode in the life of Christ presents Jesus as most appealing or inspiring to you and, therefore, in a manner that evokes within you a strong desire to devote yourself to him and to his mission.

Scripture: The entire Gospel of Mark or any three or four chapters of it; or if you prefer, one of the other three Gospels, or any three or four chapters of them.

Your Response:

❖ Begin with Preparatory Prayer, asking for help to attain the objective of the exercise. Example: "Dear Father, open my mind and heart as I consider the marvelous character qualities of Jesus. Enable me to be led by Your Holy Spirit. I ask in Jesus' name. Amen."

✛ Without diminishing the value of any of the incidents in the life of Jesus, determine what episode in the life of Christ presents Jesus as most appealing or inspiring to you. Do this by reading through the Gospel of Mark or any other Gospel. Speed-read some paragraphs, merely glance at others, but read thoughtfully the ones that portray Jesus in a manner that evokes within you a strong desire to devote yourself to him and to his mission. Use your imagination to picture the scenes if that helps. Time limitations and your familiarity with the Gospels will affect how many chapters you read. It is helpful to use a Bible with paragraph divisions or titles such as are found in *The New International Version, The New King James Version,* the *New Revised Standard Version, The Jerusalem Bible, The Orthodox Study Bible,* the *Good News Bible,* and *The New Living Bible.*

✛ You will probably come up with three or four episodes that reveal qualities of Jesus that are impressive to you. Discern which episode portrays the one quality of Christ that challenges, consoles, or inspires you the most. This is not supposed to be an intellectual exercise. Instead, try to be sensitive to your emotional response to the person of Christ. Be influenced by your feelings of attraction to and love for Jesus.

✛ Seek to be aware of Heart Prayer by being conscious of consolations: peace, joy, sadness, confidence, praise, urge for self-giving, or adoration. Stay with your emotions as long they continue, then offer thanks and praise to God for the gift of Heart Prayer. It is an indication that the Lord is enabling you to enter into the prayer exercise with your heart as well as your head.

✛ Having identified the primary character quality in Jesus that appeals to you, ask him in a Prayer of Petition for a greater desire to become more like him in that regard. Then, express your love and admiration to the Lord through the Prayer of Adoration.

✢ Conclude your time of prayer by engaging for a few minutes in the Prayer of Rest, sitting quietly in the presence of Christ who loves you just as you are and promises to be with you always (Matthew 28:20; Hebrews 13:5).

Day Two: "The Word Became Flesh"

<u>Objective</u>: Intimate knowledge of Christ that I might be *with* him, become *like* him, and live *for* him.

<u>Scripture</u>: John 1:1-18.

<u>First point</u>: The Word, God, and creation.

<u>Second point</u>: The Word and John the Baptist.

<u>Third point</u>: The Word becomes human, full of grace and truth.

Your Response:

✢ Begin with Preparatory Prayer, seeking God's help to attain the objective of the exercise.

✢ Use Meditative Reading as the prayer mode for this exercise. Try reading the text out loud giving emphasis to important words or phrases. Consider the first point as thoroughly as you can. Then move on to the second point and then to the third. Remember that in Meditative Reading you approach the text with patient humility, waiting for words, phrases, and ideas to make their impact on you. Or you can think of Meditative Reading as a shifting back and forth like a sonar technician listening for a contact point. As you are impressed with words or thoughts, pause and weigh their significance.

✢ Stay with and draw from the emotions they evoke. Experience those feelings fully; respond to their challenge.

✢ Enter into the Prayer of Adoration by thanking and praising God for any increase in knowledge of Christ that inspires you to love and serve him more fully. Savor this knowledge of Christ. Invite the Holy Spirit to intensify your appreciation of Jesus as you adore him. Then, rest in his presence and

51

commune with him for a few minutes in the Prayer of Rest. Return to adoration when your mind wanders, and then go back again to the Prayer of Rest.

✜ As you review your prayer period, consider how well you achieved the objective of the prayer exercise. Did you experience intimate knowledge of Christ? Did you sense that you were *with* Christ during the exercise and that you were with him in a more intentional way during the Prayer of Rest? Did you have a desire within you to become more *like* Christ as a result of beholding the glory of the Lord (2 Corinthians 3:18)? Did you conclude your session by giving yourself in service *for* the Lord? If not, take a moment to do that: offer yourself as a living sacrifice, holy and pleasing to God — this is your spiritual act of worship (Romans 12:1-2).

Day Three: *"Annunciation and Visitation"*

<u>Objective</u>: Intimate knowledge of Christ that I might be *with* him, become *like* him, and live *for* him.

<u>Scripture</u>: Luke 1:26-56.

<u>First point</u>: Gabriel's salutation and announcement.

<u>Second point</u>: Mary's response to Gabriel.

<u>Third point</u>: Elizabeth's and her unborn child's response to Mary; *Mary's Song.*

Your Response:

✜ Begin with Preparatory Prayer.

✜ You may want to center your thinking and enter into this exercise by turning to one or more of the traditional Christmas carols, singing joyously to the Lord.

✜ Using the Prayer of Imaginative Contemplation, visualize the points listed above. Carefully go over the Scripture passage. Let it come alive by engaging your sense of sight, sound, smell, touch, and taste. If you think that you are not a creative or artistic person and cannot pray this way because you have little imagination, realize that every time you picture the face of a friend in your mind's eye — however hazy the features — you are using the same faculties as those that are necessary to pray imaginatively.

As you imagine this scene, step into the story and become part of the action. Sense the excitement of Mary. Watch her demeanor. Value her humility as she responds to Gabriel. Join Elizabeth in giving praise to God for the blessing that he is providing through Mary. Interact with these extraordinary women by imagining their fears, hopes, and dreams. Then discuss your fears, hopes, and dreams with Christ.

Your feelings of peace, joy, sadness, confidence, praise, urge for self-giving, or adoration are indicators of what the Holy Spirit wants you to notice. Stay with these feelings, recognizing them as lovely gifts from the Lord. After the emotions subside, thank him for giving you the opportunity to enter the narrative with your heart.

Seek to find one impression or insight that you can grasp profoundly and which will lead to intimate knowledge of God that you might know, love, and serve him more fully. Ask yourself, "What does this text reveal about God's wisdom, resources, or plan that moves me to praise and thank God?"

❖ Engage in the Prayer of Adoration, thanking and adoring the Lord for an increase in the knowledge of God which enables you to love and serve him more fully. Then, for several minutes, become quiet in the Lord's presence in the Prayer of Rest.

❖ Among the things you may want to consider as you review your prayer exercises might be this question: Did you seek to dwell on one thing deeply?

Day Four: "Jesus' Birth"

Objective: Intimate knowledge of Christ that I might be *with* him, become *like* him, and live *for* him.

Scripture: Luke 2:1-20.

<u>First point</u>: Mary and Joseph go from Nazareth to Bethlehem; the birth, the swaddling clothes, the manger.

<u>Second point</u>: The angel, heavenly host, and praise of God.

<u>Third point</u>: The shepherds find Mary and Joseph and the babe lying in a manger. The shepherds return glorifying and praising God.

Your Response:

- ❖ Begin with Preparatory Prayer.

- ❖ To enter into the joy and sacredness of the birth of Christ, it may be helpful to turn to one or more of your favorite Christmas carols and sing reverently to the Lord.

- ❖ Use Meditative Reading as the prayer mode for this meditation. Try reading the text several times out loud. This can help you become sensitive to the significance of the words, especially as you read certain words or phrases or paragraphs several times, changing your tone or inflection to emphasize significant points. Try to sense the importance of the angel's announcement. Seek to enter into the joy of the shepherds, of Mary, and of Joseph. Be aware of and stay with any consolation given to you by the Spirit (such as, peace, love, trust, praise, and adoration).

  Meditate on the words, phrases, or thoughts that impress you, disturb you, or inspire you. Interact with the Lord after each verse or two. Tell him what you notice. Invite him to give you insight. Ask him any questions you have. Pause to listen for his response. This often comes in the form of an insight that touches both mind and heart.

- ❖ Offer a Prayer of Petition if the passage speaks to you of a personal, professional, or family need that requires the Lord's assistance.

- ❖ Engage in the Prayer of Adoration by thanking and praising God for any increase in the knowledge of Christ. Then quietly abide in his presence for several minutes in the Prayer of Rest.

Day Five: "The Boy Jesus at the Temple"

<u>Objective</u>: Intimate knowledge of Christ that I might be *with* him, become *like* him, and live *for* him.

<u>Scripture</u>: Luke 2:41-50.

<u>First point</u>: At age twelve Jesus goes from Nazareth to Jerusalem.

<u>Second point</u>: Jesus remains in Jerusalem. His parents do not know it.

<u>Third point</u>: After three days his parents find him in the temple. They ask him why he stayed behind and he responds.

Your Response:

❖ Begin with Preparatory Prayer.

❖ Use Imaginative Contemplation as you meditate on this story. Picture the trip to Jerusalem, the return toward Nazareth, the realization of Jesus' absence. Notice the rubbish on the streets of Jerusalem left by the Passover crowds. Smell the fresh bread being baked in the homes next to the road. Sense the anxiety of Joseph as he searches for Jesus. Place yourself in the Temple scene. Hear the quiet echo of Jesus' voice as he asks questions of the teachers.

❖ Take this opportunity to ask Jesus any questions that you may have for him. He is the Teacher who gives light to every person. Following each question, sit quietly before him and listen for his response. You may want to record your questions and also the thoughts that come to you and the impressions or feelings you experience as you wait for the Lord's answer. Thank him for the opportunity to interact with him.

❖ Offer Prayers of Petition that seem appropriate. Then, sit in the Lord's presence for a few minutes in the Prayer of Rest.

❖ Review your prayer exercise using the review suggestions offered for Days Two or Three. Among the things you may want to consider will be whether you were sensitive to Heart Prayer and whether you gave thanks to God for it.

Day Six: "Repeat"

Use this *"Repeat"* prayer period to return to any previous exercise that seemed promising but that you had to cut short. Or, you may want to go back to a prayer exercise you missed. Another option that I recommend highly is to return to a prayer exercise that went well to see what more the Holy Spirit has for you there.

Day Seven: "Review"

Use "Review" to go over all of the prayer exercises you have had this week. Often the Lord will speak a distinct word to us throughout the week, or perhaps for several weeks, to draw our attention to a special need in our lives. For many, this can be the most rewarding of all of the seven sessions. Proceed by reviewing your journal or notes, or by going back to each exercise, checking to see whether the Lord provided a common message. Or you may want to return to those insights that gave you consolation. Seek to enter into the joy of the truths and images that drew you to a more intimate knowledge of yourself and Jesus. This period of review is intended to be a savoring of the whole week.

FRIENDS ON THE JOURNEY

Bob — Awareness of feelings

After Bob had read my comments on "Heart Prayer," he wanted to talk about the emotions he had experienced in Week 1 during the "Solace" meditation on the Prodigal Son. He had used Imaginative Contemplation and when he "saw" himself safe within the Father's arms, he felt "an overwhelming sense of love beyond description." He experienced deeply felt sobs and weeping. He was conscious of his emotions and stayed with them, feeling deep gratitude to God for always welcoming him home no matter how many times he had strayed.

I thanked Bob for sharing this experience and agreed with him that Heart Prayer can be very valuable. As much as I appreciate hearing about the insights that people receive in prayer, I am more interested in hearing about their experiences of Heart Prayer. That's because Heart

Prayer generally has greater power to bond a person to God. I urged Bob to continue to take notice of the consolations that came to him, explaining that those feelings would be unique to his experience of God and would attach him ever more closely to the Lord.

At the same time, I cautioned Bob against the common tendency of making grand promises to God while experiencing deep, positive emotions. For example, some people, inspired by consolations, pledge that they will devote themselves to an hour of prayer every morning for the rest of their lives. When consolations subside, as they inevitably do, the likelihood of fulfilling this ambitious promise is close to nil, since it was most likely inspired by emotions rather than by the Holy Spirit.

Cathy — Other spiritual input

Cathy commented that in addition to the prayer project, she was reading spiritual books, listening to preachers on audio cassette tapes, and planning to sign up for a weekend retreat.

I affirmed her desire to get close to the Lord, but pointed out that this prayer project could be compromised by other devotional practices. This happens in sports when tennis lessons in the morning and a weight training program in the afternoon wear a person out for a swimming lesson in the evening. I urged her to focus on one thing at a time, especially in the early stages of learning the new skills in this prayer program. The methods of prayer described in Week 2 and the four types of insights introduced in Week 3 take time to be grasped and applied. They can be learned only through practice. The adage is true: only by praying does one learn to pray.

With equal emphasis, I also wanted to assure Cathy that worship experiences with other Christians are highly compatible with Devotional Prayer. Private, personal prayer is extremely important, but it cannot stand alone in the spiritual life. I encouraged Cathy to attend Sunday worship services, as well as other praise, fellowship, or Bible study services during the week. These *public* congregational events would strengthen and balance her *private* devotional prayer life.

WEEK 3

DELIGHTING IN THE LORD

We go to the Scriptures eager to hear the Lord's word to us, and there are days when one insight after another leaps from the page until we shake our heads in amazement over the richness of God's communication. Our intention is to dwell deeply on one thing, but we find three or four points of interest competing for our attention.

A way to resolve this happy dilemma is to identify each insight according to one of four types: Principle Insight (P), Attachment Insight (A), Interior Insight (I), or Detachment Insight (D). I will be describing these four major insights, and will be indicating that Attachment Insights (A), which reveal some aspect of the greatness and goodness of God, are generally the most beneficial. They, especially, have the power to lead us to a deeper devotion and delight in the Lord.

FOUR TYPES OF INSIGHTS

When praying over a Bible passage, I find it helpful to pause and consider the thoughts that catch my interest. This enables me to determine which ideas, insights, or themes are most significant for me. Most of the insights that grab my attention can be placed into one of the following four categories:

Principle Insight (P)

A Principle Insight (P) is one that expresses a comprehensive and fundamental truth relating to the spiritual life. It answers the question: "Is there a universal truth in this passage?" A Principle Insight (P) may be drawn from a parable or a story, or it can be found in a Bible verse as in the verses below.

Examples of verses leading to Principle Insights (P):

- "If you believe, you will receive whatever you ask for" (Matthew 21:22).

- "For everyone who exalts himself will be humbled, and he who humbles himself will be exalted" (Luke 14:11).

- "Whoever can be trusted with very little can also be trusted with much, and whoever is dishonest with very little will also be dishonest with much" (Luke 16:10).

These statements express fundamental laws or general principles relating to the spiritual life. During our prayer exercises, we might find ourselves drawn to a statement like one of these. After identifying it as a Principle Insight (P), we may want to consider the degree to which the principle is pertinent to our life situation. If we feel that it has special applicability to us, we could spend time pondering it and asking the Lord for guidance on how to apply its wisdom, teaching, or warning to our lives.

Attachment Insight (A)

An Attachment Insight (A) is one that draws us closer to God by revealing something of God's greatness. An Attachment Insight (A) answers the question: "What in the text inspires me to love God more?" You know that you have an Attachment Insight when you notice something about God that makes you say "WOW! What a mighty (or wonderful, or compassionate, or wise) God we serve!"

Examples of verses leading to Attachment Insights (A):

- "Filled with compassion, Jesus reached out his hand and touched the man. 'I am willing,' he said, 'Be clean!'" (Mark 1:41).

As you imagine Jesus reaching out, touching, and healing the man with the disease of leprosy, you may be strongly impressed with his compassion, power to heal, accessibility, responsiveness, or some other quality. The personal trait or quality of Jesus that inspires you most would be your Attachment Insight (A).

- "Heaven and earth will pass away, but my words will never pass away" (Luke 21:33).

Under the inspiration of the Spirit, you may find yourself rejoicing, perhaps ecstatically, over the durability of the words of Jesus. The Attachment Insight (A) in that case would be the imperishable nature of

Jesus' words. (Notice that Luke 21:33 also qualifies as a Principle Insight (P).)

- "This is my body given for you. This cup is the new covenant in my blood, which is poured out for you" (Luke 22:19-20).

Meditation on this passage may lead to an Attachment Insight (A) having to do with the depth of Jesus' love and sacrifice.

Interior Insight (I)

Knowledge of God and knowledge of self are both essential in the spiritual life. An Interior Insight (I) provides an increase in self-understanding: our hidden motivations, deepest aspirations, gifts, emotional needs, hidden sins, strengths, and who we are in Christ. This kind of insight helps us affirm positive qualities in our lives, brings us face to face with deficiencies needing change, and helps us identify the call of God on our lives. An Interior Insight (I) answers the question: "What in this text helps me to see and know myself as I really am?"

Examples of verses leading to Interior Insights (I):

- "But Zacchaeus stood up and said to the Lord, 'Look, Lord! Here and now I give half of my possessions to the poor, and if I have cheated anybody out of anything I will pay back four times the amount'" (Luke 19:8).

The response of Zacchaeus to Jesus' friendship helped an individual realize how God's forgiving grace toward her had released a similar flow of generosity within her. That Interior Insight (I) helped her understand that contributing to the needs of others was God's solemn call on her life.

- "Put on the new self, created to be like God in true righteousness and holiness" (Ephesians 4:24).

While meditating on this passage, an individual became acutely aware of his new identity in Christ and of God's expectation that he live a righteous and holy life.

- "As he taught for false christs and false prophets will appear and perform signs and miracles to deceive the elect — if that were possible. So be on your guard; I have told you everything ahead of time" (Mark 13:22-23).

This passage helped a person recognize that he was overly impressed with miracle workers. The text served as a flashing red light, warning him of his vulnerability in this area.

Detachment Insight (D)

A Detachment Insight (D) instructs us to rid ourselves of those affections that prove a hindrance to wholehearted devotion to God. Ignatius called those affections "inordinate attachments" and indicated that a major purpose of the Spiritual Exercises was to prepare and dispose an individual to rid him or her "of all inordinate attachments, and, after their removal, [to seek] and [find] the will of God."[1] A Detachment Insight (D) answers the question: "How does this text instruct me to deny myself and to take up my cross?" (Luke 9:23).

Examples of verses leading to Detachment Insights (D):

- "When someone invites you to a wedding feast, do not take the place of honor, for a person more distinguished than you may have been invited" (Luke 14:8).

A Detachment Insight (D) suggested by this verse is the need to detach yourself from self-exaltation; or, perhaps, from the presumption that you are better than others.

- "And when you stand praying, if you hold anything against anyone, forgive him, so that your Father in heaven may forgive you your sins" (Mark 11:25).

A Detachment Insight (D) would lead you to repent of an unforgiving spirit towards someone against whom you have held a grudge.

- "As he taught, Jesus said, 'Watch out for the teachers of the law. They like to walk around in flowing robes and be greeted in the marketplaces, and have the most important seats in the synagogues and the places of honor at banquets. And they devour widows' houses and for a show make lengthy prayers'" (Mark 12:38-40a).

The inappropriate affections suggested by this passage include the use of gaudy clothing, the desire for preferential treatment, the practice of unscrupulous financial dealings, and the insincerity of offering lengthy prayers designed to impress others. The Spirit could direct your attention to any of these common faults and convict you of the need to repent and to develop an attitude of detachment from them.

Further instruction on when and how to search for and benefit from the four types of insights will be included in the "Your Response" comments within the prayer exercises.

Preferring Attachment Insights

Delighting in the Lord through Attachment Insights (A) is a top priority in Devotional Prayer. Dallas Willard, describing how people are developed into disciples of Jesus, explained that this happens when people find Jesus "so admirable in every respect — wise, beautiful, powerful, and good — that they constantly seek to be in his presence and be guided, instructed, and helped by him in every aspect of their lives."[2]

Without using my terminology, Dallas Willard was talking about the importance of focusing on Attachment Insights (A). It is inevitable that our love for Christ will grow as we make "one great volitional act," as A. W. Tozer advised, "which establishes the heart's intention to gaze forever upon Jesus."[3] As we take notice of the grace and wisdom of Jesus and listen to his words, ponder them, and apply them to our lives, we find a responsive love growing within us. This leads us to greater devotion for Christ and a greater determination to be like him and to serve him. It is for these reasons that I urge you to develop a preference for Attachment Insights (A).

If we place so high a priority on Attachment Insights, you may wonder why we bother with the other three types. We must do so because the spiritual life is complex. It needs the benefit of all four types of insights.

Take, for example, Principle Insights (P). Jesus frequently communicated Kingdom values by stating principles, as he did when he was being arrested. One of his disciples, Peter, used violence to resist the arrest of Jesus, cutting off the ear of the servant of the high priest with a sword. But Jesus told Peter to put his sword back in its place, and then added, "all who draw the sword will die by the sword" (Matthew 26:52). Jesus was expressing an important principle: violence begets violence. Jesus then transformed the potentially homicidal act into a teachable moment by healing the servant's ear (Luke 22:51). The words of Jesus carried greater weight as a result of his act of mercy.

Among other things, this episode teaches that we need to know biblical principles well enough to be able to communicate them at will, as Jesus did, so that we can teach important values to others.

Jesus also helped individuals gain self-understanding which is what an Interior Insight (I) accomplishes. Think of the resurrected Lord asking Peter three times whether Peter loved him. Peter would never forget that interview because it took him back to the night he had denied the Lord. Jesus had told Peter and the other disciples that they would scatter and abandon him, but Peter had emphatically insisted that he never would, even if all the others fell away (Matthew 26:33). Yet Peter wound up denying the Lord three times. Jesus reminded Peter of that tragic scene because Peter needed to grasp not only the depth of the forgiveness and love of Jesus but also Peter's obsessive tendency to place his confidence in his own strength and abilities. That was important self-understanding. Peter needed to guard against that tendency if he was to fulfill God's call on his life to feed Christ's lambs and tend Christ's sheep (John 21).

Detachment Insights (D) are obviously important since Jesus made detachment a condition of discipleship: "If anyone would come after me, he must deny himself and take up his cross and follow me" (Matthew 16:24). The Spirit knows the extent to which we are attached to anger, rage, malice, slander, filthy speech, sexual immorality, impurity, lust, and greed. These things, which belong to our old self (Colossians 3:5-9), need to be put to death. If they are not, we will find ourselves bound by them, lacking the spiritual freedom to follow Jesus.

John Calvin had as his first rule of correct prayer a "devout detachment"[4] from carnal cares and thoughts by which one's mind could be called or led away from right and pure contemplation of God. He recognized that this would not be an easy thing to do, but counseled that we ought to labor strenuously to achieve it, and be grateful for the Holy Spirit given to us by God because the Spirit helps us to pray as we ought.

Choosing the "Right" Insight

Since all four types of insights can be helpful, how do you choose one over the others? You do it by the Spirit's direction, and this requires a carefully honed sensitivity. At times you will have an Attachment Insight (A) and a Detachment Insight (D) that both seem important, but the Detachment Insight may seem more pressing, more urgent. Under those circumstances you should focus your attention on the Detachment Insight and ask the Lord for understanding and help in applying it to your life.

If on the other hand you have several insights competing for your attention with none standing out in any special way, you would be wise to give preference to the Attachment Insight (A). It has greater potential for increasing your devotion to God and thus enabling you to fulfill the first commandment.

The mistake many people make is to bypass Attachment Insights or even fail to notice them in favor of one of the other types of insights. I have noticed, for example, that pastors and teachers gravitate toward Principle Insights (P), probably because there is constant pressure for them to come up with something that will "preach" or that can be taught clearly and easily. But the power of the pulpit or lectern is diminished by excessive concentration on spiritual principles, especially when the vastly more powerful, attractive, and beneficial themes of the person and work of Jesus are neglected. Furthermore, the pastor, lay leader, or church member who focuses on Principle Insights (P) instead of Attachment Insights (A) will not experience the same degree of delight in the Lord or intimacy with the Lord during his or her prayer time. Nor will the reality of Christ's love and presence shine through the pastor's or lay leader's preaching or teaching as when he or she gives preference to Attachment Insights.

PRAYER RESPONSE SHEET

For those persons who desire a more orderly way of making notes as they progress through their prayer period, I have included a "Prayer Response Sheet" (shown on p. 67). By duplicating it, you can use one copy for each prayer period. The Prayer Response Sheet provides opportunity for you to note the types of prayer you offered, the insights you received, and the responses you made to the review questions. It provides the benefit of self-administered feedback at the conclusion of the prayer period.

By filling out the sheet on a regular basis, you will become more conscious of such things as centering (preparing yourself for prayer) and focusing on the objective of the prayer exercise (by rating how well you did on a scale of 1 to 5). You will also become more proficient in identifying the various prayer modes you experienced and the insights you received. The Response Sheet will also ask you to consider the beneficial or distracting elements that helped or hindered your prayer session. Because the feedback can be immediate and specific, the Prayer Response Sheet serves as an effective training tool.

You will notice that I have used the acrostic "P" "A" "I" "D" to help you remember the four types of insights. The term reminds us that Jesus released us from guilt and delivered us from slavery to sin because Jesus PAID the ransom for us. As Romans 3:23-25a teaches:

> *All have sinned and fall short of the glory of God, and are justified freely by his grace through the redemption that came by Christ Jesus. God presented him as a sacrifice of atonement, through faith in his blood.*

In the NIV Study Bible footnote for Romans 3:24, Walter W. Wessell comments: "Paul uses this word [redemption] to refer to release from guilt, with its liability for judgment, and to deliverance from slavery to sin, because Christ in his death *paid* [italics added] the ransom for us."

One might ask, "Paid to whom? To God? Is God a sadist?" The answer is "NO!" In giving his Son, God gave himself. As the distinguished theologian, Karl Barth, reasoned:

> Because it was the Son of God, *i.e.,* God himself, who took our place on Good Friday, the substitution could be effectual and procure our reconciliation with the righteous God.... Only God, our Lord and Creator, could stand surety for us, could take our place, could suffer eternal death in our stead as the consequence of our sin in such a way that it was finally suffered and overcome.[5]

PRAYER RESPONSE SHEET*

Date: _____ Week/Day: _____

Prayer Exercise: _____

Time: _____ Location: _____

How did I center? _____

Objective (for most prayer exercises): Intimate knowledge of Christ that I might be *with* him, become *like* him, and live *for* him.

Prayer Modes: Preparatory Prayer (p. 41)
                          Mental Prayer:
                                  Meditative Reading (p. 42)
                                  Imaginative Contemplation (p. 43)
                                  Prayer of Consideration (p. 44)
                          Heart Prayer (p. 44)
                          Prayer of Petition (p. 46)
                          Prayer of Adoration (p. 47)
                          Prayer of Rest (p. 47)

Insights:

P   Principle: "Is there a universal truth?"

A   Attachment: "What inspires me to love Christ more?"

I   Interior: "What helps me know myself as I really am?"

D   Detachment: "How does this instruct me to deny myself?"

Review Assessment:

Objective achieved? Scale of one to five _____

What was my "feeling state"? (Peaceful, joyous, dry, restless, etc.)

Was there a special Prayer of Petition I would like to record?

Did I enter into the Prayer of Adoration? The Prayer of Rest?

Did I offer yourself in service *for* the Lord?

What proved to be helpful or distracting?

*Reproduction of this page is authorized.

SEVEN PRAYER EXERCISES

The "Prayer Exercises" this week include four very significant meditations on the early stages of Jesus' ministry: *"Baptism,"* *"Temptation,"* *"Water to Wine,"* and *"Samaritan Woman."* The objective of each of these prayer exercises and most of those in the coming weeks will be to gain "Intimate knowledge of Christ that I might be *with* him, become *like* him, and live *for* him." In addition, you will find one of Ignatius' challenging, thematic spiritual exercises called *"Two Banners."*[6] This prayer exercise helps you identify and embrace the values characteristic of Christ and identify and turn away from the values characteristic of the evil one. The sixth and seventh prayer exercises are *"Repeat"* and *"Review"* opportunities.

Day One: "Baptism"

Objective: Intimate knowledge of Christ that I might be *with* him, become *like* him, and live *for* him.

Scripture: Matthew 3:13-17.

First point: Jesus comes from Galilee to the river Jordan to be baptized by John.

Second point: The dialogue between John and Jesus and the baptism of Jesus.

Third point: The Holy Spirit descends; the Father speaks.

Your Response:

✣ Ask the Lord to help you achieve the objective of this prayer exercise by using a Preparatory Prayer. Example: "Dear Lord Jesus, please open your word to me by your Holy Spirit. Enable me to know you more intimately that I might commune with you, become more like you, and offer myself in service for you. I ask this in your holy name. Amen."

✣ Using the prayer of Imaginative Contemplation, visualize the baptism in your mind's eye. Call upon your five senses as you move from point to point. For example, what was the expression on John's face and what was the tone of his voice as he said, "I need to be baptized by you, and do you come to me?" What did the water feel like as Jesus went into it and taste like when he came up out of it? What was distinctive in the voice that said, "This is my Son, whom I love; with him I am well pleased"?

✢   As you go back and imagine the scene a second time, look for an Attachment Insight (A). Ask yourself, "What in the text causes me to admire, appreciate, or love Christ more?" This virtue of Christ can be something that you have often admired in the past, yet the Spirit may use this scene to provide a new depth of appreciation. If there are several Attachment Insights (A), use the Prayer of Petition to ask the Holy Spirit to impress upon you the one that he wants you to dwell upon most fully. This is in accordance with Ignatius' counsel that "it is not much knowledge that fills and satisfies the soul, but the intimate understanding and the relish of the truth."[7]   Feel free to follow any other truths or insights beyond Attachment Insights (A). Try to stay flexible so that you can follow the Holy Spirit's lead.

✢   Be conscious of any positive emotions that you may feel during the prayer exercise (peace, joy, sadness, confidence, praise, urge for self-giving, adoration, etc.). These emotions, if they are stirred by the text and if they lead you closer to the Lord, are most likely Heart Prayer. If you are experiencing this kind of prayer, invite the Lord to intensify the emotions (Prayer of Petition). Stay with the emotions as long as they last. Recognize that consolation is a lovely gift from the Lord. After your feelings subside, thank him for this gift.

✢   Assuming that you have been led to an Attachment Insight (A) that has given you intimate knowledge of Christ, take a few moments to offer praise and gratitude to him in the Prayer of Adoration. Then sit humbly and gratefully in his presence for a few moments in the Prayer of Rest. The combination of the Prayer of Adoration and the Prayer of Rest works well together. If your mind wanders, don't be rough on yourself. Bring your thoughts back *gently* by returning to your Attachment Insight (A), which returns you to adoration. Then move back again to abiding in Christ in the Prayer of Rest. The time of rest with Christ is very significant. It builds faith, hope, and love.

✢ Conclude your prayer exercise by offering yourself in service *for* Christ. Seek to do this in a way that comes from the depths of your heart. Repeat your offering several times.

✢ Review your prayer exercise by asking yourself whether any of the activities you engaged in during this meditation hindered or helped. Or you may want to use the more structured and comprehensive "Prayer Response Sheet" with its list of review assessment questions (see p. 67).

Day Two: "Temptation"

Objective: Intimate knowledge of Christ that I might be *with* him, become *like* him, and live *for* him.

Scripture: Matthew 4:1-11.

First point: After baptism, Jesus went into the desert where he fasted for 40 days and nights.

Second point: The three temptations of the enemy.

Third point: Jesus answered each temptation with Scripture.

Your Response:

✢ Begin with Preparatory Prayer, asking for God's help to achieve the objective of this prayer exercise. A stanza from a familiar hymn can sometimes be a helpful aide for centering (p. 25). Take, for example, the fourth stanza from *Break Thou the Bread of Life*: "O send Thy Spirit, Lord, now unto me, that he may touch my eyes and make me see; show me the truth concealed within thy word, for in thy book revealed I see thee, Lord. Amen."

✢ Use the Prayer of Consideration in this meditation. Ask the Lord to help you come up with Principle Insights (P). They answer the question: "Is there a universal spiritual truth being expressed in this passage?" During most of this prayer period, your concentration will probably be on the second point (the three temptations of the enemy).

❖ If you identify several Principle Insights (P), use the Prayer of Petition to ask the Lord to lead you to the insight most relevant for you. Take time to think about the insight, weighing the pros and cons of it, relating it to your conduct and activities.

❖ Consider which insight best enables you to achieve the objective of the prayer exercise ("Intimate knowledge of Christ ..."). Is it the same as the one chosen in the previous step? Does the Lord want you to change to the one that supports the objective or does he want you to stick with the one that satisfies your current needs? Only you can answer. Remember he leads through peace. In which choice do you sense more of the Lord's peace? Don't be troubled if you aren't certain. You will develop sensitivity as you gain experience.

❖ You will find so much in this passage that could easily lead you to Attachment Insights (A), Interior Insights (I), or Detachment Insights (D). If you are led to consider any of these, feel free to go with them. I am stressing Principle Insights (P) for this meditation so that you can develop ease in identifying this type of insight.

❖ Assuming that you have been led to a Principle Insight (P) that has given you a better understanding of Christ and has stimulated a genuine love for him and a desire to serve him, express that love in the Prayer of Adoration. Then, commune with the Lord by gratefully resting in his presence for a few minutes in the Prayer of Rest. As you attempt to quiet yourself, do not be surprised or agitated if you find yourself confronted with various distractions. Be gentle with yourself and return to your Principle Insight (P) or whichever insight was most significant for you. Then release that insight and rest in the Lord's presence.

❖ Following the Prayer of Rest, conclude your prayer exercise by thanking the Lord for giving you intimate knowledge of himself and for communing with you. Make a point of offering yourself in service for Christ.

❖ Review your prayer period by considering these questions: Were you able to dwell deeply upon one insight? Were you able to experience the Lord's presence at a deeper level during your Prayer of Rest? Did you go beyond being informed of God's will to being energized to do it? Don't be discouraged if you cannot answer all these questions affirmatively. Use the Prayer of Petition to ask the Lord to help you. He will.

Day Three: "Water to Wine"

Objective: Intimate knowledge of Christ that I might be *with* him, become *like* him, and live *for* him.

Scripture: John 2:1-11.

First point: Christ and his disciples were invited to a wedding.

Second point: Mary's comments.

Third point: Jesus changed water to wine, thereby revealing his glory. His disciples put their faith in him.

Your Response:

❖ Begin with Preparatory Prayer.

❖ Use Meditative Reading as the prayer mode for this exercise. As you go over the text, read the verses (preferably out loud) using variation in tone or inflection. Ponder the words, phrases, or verses that catch your attention. Talk to the Lord about these words or phrases and ask how they might relate to your life. Also, be conscious of any consolations that you may feel (delight, sorrow, trust, devotion, or urge for self-giving), and enter into them as fully as you can, giving thanks to God for them.

❖ After you have savored a word or idea that the Lord has drawn to your attention, consider what type of insight it might be: Principle (P), Attachment (A), Interior (I), or Detachment (D). Remember that with Meditative Reading, you do not search for insights. Instead, you allow the words of Scripture to impact you as you read them with openness and receptivity. After you have been impressed by a certain thought or word, you will process that thought further by considering the type of insight it might be. This differs from the way in which you proceed with the Prayer of Consideration. With it, you move into the Scripture intentionally searching for specific insights.

❖ Enter into the Prayer of Adoration by thanking and praising God for any increase in knowledge of Christ that inspires you to love and serve him more fully. Allow this knowledge of Christ to warm your heart, as you adore him. Also, use the Prayer of Petition to request that the Lord conform you to the qualities he exhibited in this story. Then, rest in his presence and commune with him for a few minutes in the Prayer of Rest. If your mind wanders, bring your thoughts back by returning to your Attachment Insight and the adoration it inspires. Then let adoration go and rest in the Lord.

❖ Conclude your prayer exercise by seeking to make a deep offering of yourself to Christ.

❖ Review this prayer exercise to determine what you did that was beneficial or detrimental. The positive elements you will want to repeat in future prayer exercises. The negative elements you will want to avoid.

Day Four: "Two Banners"

<u>Objective</u>: Deeper knowledge of Christ's ways and a greater desire to imitate him on the one hand and deeper knowledge of Satan's deceits and a greater determination to guard against him.

<u>Scripture</u>: 1 Timothy 6:3-21; Philippians 2:1-18; Mark 10:35-45.

<u>Background</u>: Both Christ and Satan want us to follow their methods and promote their values. Who will lead is in the balance. Christ's banner guides us to peace and service, whereas Satan's banner leads to fear and hostility.

<u>First point</u>: It is Satan's desire to lead us into darkness and oppression by tempting us with money, praise, and power. His strategy is to tempt us to seek primarily our prosperity and well-being and to acquire a luxurious lifestyle or other trophies or accomplishments that bring

esteem from the world. Praise from others in turn leads to false pride, by which we think we deserve power and the right to fulfill all desires. We thereby become more susceptible to anger, malice, lust, and all other vices.

Second point: Jesus, on the other hand, desires to liberate us. He invites us to embrace a simplified lifestyle that we might focus on that which is truly important: being *with* him. As Christ's companions, we identify with the values and goals of Jesus and increasingly turn away from seeking material success and social standing. As a result, we sense that we do not quite "fit in" as we once did, and even find ourselves being criticized or rejected. This helps us realize that we are becoming more *like* Christ who humbled himself and suffered persecution unto death. We, in turn, desire to humble ourselves and to live in the truth of our identity as persons who are redeemed, forgiven, and sustained by Jesus. Indeed, we find that our deepest joy is being *with* Christ and giving ourselves in committed service *for* Christ.

Hence, Christ invites us to choose three dispositions: the first, simplicity; the second, humility; and the third, generosity in service. From these three dispositions, Jesus leads us to all other virtues.

Your Response:

- ❖ Use Preparatory Prayer to ask for enlightenment from the Lord.

- ❖ Using the Prayer of Consideration read 1 Timothy 6:3-21 in light of the First and Second points. As you interact with the Scripture and the two points, look for an Interior Insight. Ask yourself, "What in this text helps me to see and know myself as I really am?" Also look for a Detachment Insight. Ask yourself, "How does this text instruct me to deny myself and to take up my cross?" You need not make a list of responses. Rather, seek the insight that seems to be most deserving of notice.

- ❖ Repeat with Philippians 2:1-18 and/or Mark 10:35-45.

- ❖ Assuming that you have been led to an insight that gives you an increased awareness of the direction in which Christ desires to influence you, give praise to God in the Prayer of

Adoration. Conclude by gratefully and humbly resting in the Lord's presence for a few minutes in the Prayer of Rest.

✣ Let your prayer exercise culminate in thanksgiving to God for deeper knowledge of Christ's ways. Using the Prayer of Petition, ask him for a greater desire to live in simplicity (*with* Christ), humility (*like* Christ), and generosity in service (*for* Christ). Finally, thank the Lord for a deeper awareness of the deceits of the enemy and ask him for the determination and discernment to guard yourself against Satan's deceits.

Day Five: "Samaritan Woman"

Objective: Intimate knowledge of Christ that I might be *with* him, become *like* him, and live *for* him.

Scripture: John 4:4-38.

First point: Christ, tired and sitting by the well, asks for a drink.

Second point: Christ describes to the woman the water he provides, and the kind of worshipers the Father seeks.

Third point: Christ describes to the disciples the food he eats and the results it brings.

Your Response:

✣ Offer Preparatory Prayer.

✣ Using Imaginative Contemplation, visualize the scene at the well, first with the woman and then with the disciples. As you imagine this scene, look for an Attachment Insight (A). Ask yourself, "What in the text moves me to want to attach myself to Christ? What causes me to love Christ more?" Be conscious of any positive emotions.

✣ Using the Prayer of Adoration, express praise and adoration to Jesus for such qualities as his approachability and eagerness to share the great gift of eternal life. Use the Prayer of Petition to ask him to build these qualities into your life. Then, using the Prayer of Rest, commune with Jesus for several minutes.

✤   I reduced the number of response suggestions for this exercise. Were you able to proceed satisfactorily on your own? Review your prayer exercise using the "Prayer Response Sheet" (p. 67).

Day Six: "Repeat"

You can use this *"Repeat"* prayer period to return to any of the exercises you have had during the first three weeks. Perhaps you had to rush through one of your prayer exercises, or you may have missed another. The choice is yours. However, keep in mind that it is generally better to repeat those sessions where there was much light and peace rather than those that weren't fruitful the first time through.

Day Seven: "Review"

The Lord often has one message for us during the week. In fact, this common thread can continue for several weeks. Review your week of prayer exercises looking for a unifying message running through them all.

FRIENDS ON THE JOURNEY

Bob — Dealing with lust

Bob was having a difficult time resting in the Lord because of a problem with lust. His travels involved overnights in hotels, an increasing number of which promoted what he considered to be pornographic "adult entertainment" films. He was distressed to find that the film images dominated his thoughts when he closed his eyes to sense the presence of the Lord within him. Bob had tried to resist watching these films, but with limited success. He asked for help.

I expressed appreciation for his openness in wanting to discuss a very common but difficult problem, and one which conflicts directly with the goal of this prayer program: developing intimacy with Christ.

We talked for a long while and I sensed that he was not at a level of addiction that would require special assistance as in the case of those with a compulsive disorder. I shared with him some of the steps I have taken through the years that have been helpful to me. In a rambling style, I talked about the following:

First, I stressed that a person needs to become persuaded that the delight of daily communion with Christ is far, far better than the titillation of lust. I became convinced of this by meditating on the sixth beatitude that calls those blessed who are pure in heart for they will "see God" (Matthew 5:8). Intimate knowledge of Jesus that leads to communion with him cannot occur in a heart that is filled with sexual immorality, impurity, and evil desires, just as light cannot coexist with darkness. To cleanse my mind of pornographic images through confession and to be free of those images during my time of intimate communion with Christ might take anywhere from several days to several weeks. Losing intimacy with Christ for the titillation of lust was a price I did not want to pay!

Second, I realized that I had to take decisive action against every temptation toward lust. Jesus said, "If your right eye causes you to sin, gouge it out and throw it away ... (Matthew 5:29). I like the interpretation of these words of Jesus by my missionary friend and Bible commentator, (Frederick) Dale Bruner: "Be tough with yourself; be completely decisive; in moral matters immediate action is nine-tenths the cure; in sexual purity decisiveness is everything."[8]

When, for example, I received unsolicited and unwanted e-mail messages advertising a new pornographic web site, I deleted them immediately, reminding myself of their demonic origin (*"Our struggle is not against flesh and blood, but against the rulers, against the authorities, against the powers of this dark world and against the spiritual forces of evil in the heavenly realms" [Ephesians 6:12]*). I did not want the temptation to last a second longer than necessary. Swift, surgical action is necessary in this realm because the impulse toward impurity is extremely powerful.

Third, I made sure that I was finding sexual satisfaction with my wife. Giving us a marriage partner is God's normal way of enabling us to satisfy the sexual desire. The Apostle Paul urged husbands and wives not to deprive one another lest Satan tempt them (1 Corinthians 7:5). John Chrysostom advised husbands to turn their eyes and hearts and sexual desires toward home: "If thou desirest to look and find pleasure, look at thine own wife, and love her continually."[9]

77

I urged Bob to take whatever steps were necessary to purify his mind and to be vigilant in keeping it that way so that he would be able to experience the higher love of God.

Cathy — From anxiety to peace!

Cathy indicated that she had been interviewing for a new position and that this had brought an anxiety attack. Yet when she got into her prayer exercises, her fears were replaced by a quiet assurance that everything was going to be fine. She asked me to help her understand the dramatic shift in her feelings.

I smiled, urged her to give thanks to the Lord, and suggested that she review the teaching on Heart Prayer and consolation in Week 2 (pp. 44-45). I told her that God was graciously granting her the gift of peace.

I urged her to hold on to this memory for the future when she might be tested without so dramatic a rescue. The Lord wants us to be faithful in our prayers even when he doesn't give us warm and encouraging feelings. I indicated that she would receive more instruction on this topic in Week 5 where I discuss the importance of praying even when we do not experience God's peace.

WEEK 4

RESTING IN JESUS

Toward the end of your time of prayer, I usually suggest that you open your heart to God to experience the presence of the Lord at a more intimate level. Some people find this time of peaceful rest to be the most satisfying aspect of the entire prayer period. Others have difficulty entering into it. Instructions are provided in this chapter to help both groups. I also introduce "The Jesus Prayer," an ancient prayer from the Eastern Orthodox tradition that can be used along with the Prayer of Rest or in place of it.

THE PRAYER OF REST

We turn to the Prayer of Rest during the final segment of our prayer exercise. Prior to that, we engage in various forms of mental prayer that help us gather insights and increase our knowledge of God and of ourselves. We follow with prayers of petition, asking God for the help we need. Then comes a time of adoration in which we express praise for who Jesus is and for what he has done and is doing in and for us. It is at that point that we normally move to the Prayer of Rest. We enrich and complement the other ways of prayer by resting our minds and abiding in communion with the Lord.

The Prayer of Rest involves an intuitive sensing of the Lord's presence in a direct personal relationship. We commune with him in a state of intimate, heightened sensitivity and receptivity. We do this without forming pictures or analyzing concepts in our minds. Instead, we rely on faith. We affirm that the immediate presence of Christ is with us (Colossians 1:27), that we, ourselves, are at that moment dwelling in Christ, abiding in him as he abides in us (John 15:4), that we are one with Him as he is one with us and are therefore in vital union with him (John 17:21; 1 Corinthians 6:17; 12:27).

It may surprise some people to learn that evangelical Christians of significant stature, such as John Stott, believe that union with Christ is central to the New Testament Gospel. To make this point, Stott called on

79

Dr. James Stewart, who, in his *A Man in Christ,* wrote, "The heart of Paul's religion is union with Christ. This, more than any other conception — more than justification, more than sanctification, more even than reconciliation — is the key which unlocks the secrets of his soul."[1] Stewart had come to the conclusion that "in Paul's view everything is gathered up in the one great fact of communion with Christ.... Other elements of the Christian experience are not so much isolated events as aspects of the one reality, not parallel lines ... but radii of the same circle of which union with Christ is the center."[2]

Entering into the Prayer of Rest

Through the Prayer of Rest, we enter into the stillness of union with Christ, the hush of solemn silence. Scripture invites us to do this.

- *"Be still before the Lord and wait patiently for him" (Psalm 37:7).*

- *"Be still and know that I am God" (Psalm 46:10).*

- *"My presence will go with you, and I will give you rest" (Exodus 33:14).*

- *"You will keep in perfect peace him whose mind is steadfast, because he trusts in you" (Isaiah 26:3).*

- *"Peace I leave with you; my peace I give you" (John 14:27).*

- *"I have told you these things, so that in me you may have peace" (John 16:33a).*

Referring to a pebble being thrown into a quiet pond, M. Basil Pennington saw an instructive illustration on stillness. He wrote,

> When a pond is perfectly at peace and one casts a pebble into it, the gentle waves spread in every direction till they reach even the farthest shore. When we are in the midst of a busy everyday life, so many thoughts go in and out of our minds and our hearts, we do not perceive the effect they are having upon us. But when we come to achieve a deeper inner quiet, then we are much more discerning. The way is open to follow even the most gentle leadings of the Spirit and to avoid even the most subtle deviations that are suggested either by the self or by the evil one.[3]

To settle into a state of stillness is not an easy thing to do. How do we shift from prayer expressed in words to prayer experienced in silence? First, we must find a quiet setting. If we have been meditating at our desk or a table, we will find it helpful to shift to a chair that allows us to sit comfortably for a period of ten or twenty minutes. We need to be undisturbed. Closing the door of our room or unplugging a telephone will help us escape some of the common external distractions.

Second, we prepare for the Prayer of Rest by preceding it with the Prayer of Adoration offered in a thoughtful, reverent manner. Heart Prayer may and often does occur earlier in the prayer exercise, and in those moments there may be exuberant expressions of praise. But when we come to the Prayer of Adoration, we can close our eyes and bow our heads and offer praise and thanksgiving with humble respect. This helps us move into the Prayer of Rest with heightened reverence and anticipation.

Third, we must recognize by faith that the Lord Jesus lives within us and that therefore we are one with him. The head bowed toward the heart can remind us of Christ dwelling in our innermost being, symbolized by the heart. We accept the reality of his presence within by faith and can review these or other Scripture passages to reaffirm our faith:

- *"Do you not realize that Christ is in you?" (2 Corinthians 13:5)*

- *"I have been crucified with Christ and I no longer live, but Christ lives in me" (Galatians 2:20).*

- *"On that day you will realize that I am in my Father, and you are in me, and I am in you" (John 14:20).*

- *"I have made you known to them, and will continue to make you known in order that the love you have for me may be in them and that I myself may be in them" (John 17:26).*

- *"To them God has chosen to make known among the Gentiles the glorious riches of this mystery, which is Christ in you, the hope of glory" (Colossians 1:27).*

- *"Never will I leave you; never will I forsake you!" (Hebrews 13:5).*

Fourth, the three great theological virtues, "Faith," "Hope," and "Love," help us enter into the major aspects of the Prayer of Rest. *Faith* reminds us that we do not have to feel anything; instead, faith enables us to affirm that Jesus is within, awaiting our fellowship. *Hope* reminds us that the rest we find here on earth is but a partial fulfillment of our ultimate union with God. "Father, I want those you have given me to be with me where I am, to see my glory" (John 17:24). *Love* reminds us that we are in the presence of the One who loves us far beyond our ability to understand the width, length, height, and depth of his love for us (Ephesians 3:18); and, therefore, we love him in return. On the basis of these truths, we make ourselves silent in His presence, our hearts filled with *faith, hope,* and *love.*

Dealing with Distractions while in the Prayer of Rest

During the Prayer of Rest we may find random, everyday thoughts and distractions flashing through our minds. All who pray inwardly experience this problem. Thomas Keating has done excellent work in identifying such thoughts. "Thoughts," for him, is an umbrella term and includes sense perceptions, feelings, images, memories, and reflections, such as asking yourself during prayer, "What's happening?" or saying to yourself, "This peace feels great."[4]

As you become aware of thoughts, one way to deal with them would be to let them drift by like passing clouds as you gently return your mind to the presence of the Lord. Avoid becoming disappointed or frustrated with yourself. That will only agitate you and make it more difficult to rest your mind. Realize that the Lord understands, loves, and is patient with you as you draw near.

Though temporarily distracted, you can refocus on the Lord by use of a word, phrase, image, or symbol. I would recommend using the "Motivating Statement" that you were asked to come up with in Week 1. It was the word you selected in answer to the question, "What phrase, statement, image, or symbol can I use to guide me in the direction that I want my life to take?" The word or phrase you chose should help you in fulfilling your desire to be with Jesus, rest in his presence, welcome his transforming work in your heart, and be lovingly attentive to what he is doing. Use it or some other word or phrase for refocusing into the Prayer of Rest.

Once you are aware of the Lord's immediate presence, let go of thoughts and images and simply relax. As soon as another thought or image comes into your mind, gently release it, repeat your word or phrase, and allow that word to represent your desire to be in communion with Christ.

Remember that the objective in the Prayer of Rest is intimacy with Jesus. That does not necessarily mean achieving a spiritual experience or even feeling peaceful. It certainly does not mean emptying the mind or trying to make it blank. This is one way the Prayer of Rest differs from Buddhist introspection.

Infused Prayer

There are those who encourage a type of "Centering Prayer" which excludes thinking. In his book, *Open Mind, Open Heart,* Thomas Keating wrote, "When you are not thinking at all and can just not think that thought, you have it made. There is only a short step from that point to divine union."[5] The "not thinking at all" which Keating described is what I would describe as Infused Prayer. In Infused Prayer, the Lord takes over and provides a more total gift without sufficient cause and beyond our normal capacities.

This differs from the Prayer of Rest. In the Prayer of Rest, we are conscious of Christ's presence. We realize that he graciously communes with sinful persons forgiven through his vicarious, atoning sacrifice. But even as we acknowledge this great privilege, foolish and distracting thoughts can disrupt our communion with the Lord. The only way distracting thoughts are eliminated is when God grants us the gift of Infused Prayer.

How do we know when we are in Infused Prayer? The line between the Prayer of Rest and Infused Prayer is indistinct. We can be in the Prayer of Rest and, should God grant the gift of Infused Prayer, find our sense faculties mildly suspended. Without putting us to sleep, the Lord could bring us into a profound union with his will. That would be a special gift, but we would probably not be aware of being in Infused Prayer until it was over. Then, we would notice that our time in prayer passed quickly, but that we were not sleeping. Our head, for instance, did not fall to our chest as it would in sleep. We would also feel a deep sense of union with Christ or his will.

It is important to remember that the Prayer of Rest has to do with our union with God as revealed in Christ. We do not seek to go beyond the divine person, Jesus Christ. Rather, we recognize that we were created by him and for him (Colossians 1:16) and redeemed by him (Romans 3:24). We also know that he desires to enter into communion with us (John 15:4-5), while remaining the same yesterday, today, and forever (Hebrews 13:8). Thus, the Prayer of Rest relies on and has complete trust in the personal relationship that Jesus established with us through the cross. Jesus made a genuine offer of rest when he issued his gracious invitation: "Come to me, all you who are weary and burdened, and I will give you rest" (Matthew 11:28). One of the ways we appropriate this promise is through the Prayer of Rest.

THE JESUS PRAYER

Some people use the Eastern Orthodox "Jesus Prayer" as a way of coming to a deep rest in Christ. I frequently use the Jesus Prayer in conjunction with the Prayer of Rest.

The Origin of the Jesus Prayer

What is the Jesus Prayer? According to one of the foremost authorities on Eastern Orthodoxy and its spirituality, Bishop Kallistos Ware, the standard phrasing runs, *"Lord Jesus Christ, Son of God, have mercy on me."* It frequently also includes two final words, *"a sinner."* The prayer was taken from two stories in the Gospels. First is blind Bartimaeus who, upon learning that Jesus was passing by, shouted, "Jesus, Son of David, have mercy on me!" (Luke 18:38). The second is the parable of the Pharisee, who, brimming with high self-esteem, commended himself to God for not being like all other men — robbers, evildoers, adulterers, or even like the tax collector praying in the temple near him. Quite the other way, the tax collector, burdened with a sense of unworthiness, would not even look up to heaven but beat his chest and said, "God, have mercy on me, a sinner." From this, Jesus drew a startling lesson: "I tell you that this man, rather than the other, went home justified before God. For everyone who exalts himself will be humbled, and he who humbles himself will be exalted" (Luke 18:13b-14).

Influenced by the plea of blind Bartimaeus and the confession of the tax collector, the monastic communities in Egypt and Greece between the fifth and eighth centuries encountered a method of prayer that has proven deeply influential in the Christian East. It has come to be called "The Jesus Prayer."[6] There are variations to the prayer depending on the books that one examines or the Eastern Orthodox priest or monk to whom one speaks. Ware says that the one essential and unvarying element is the inclusion of the divine Name "Jesus."[7]

References to the Jesus Prayer were scattered and relatively infrequent until the fourteenth century when it was employed in the Byzantine and Slav world, but largely restricted to the monastic centers. Ware writes, "Only in our present twentieth century has it come to be adopted on a large scale by Orthodox lay people. Indeed, allowing for its contemporary popularity among Western Christians as well as Orthodox, it can be claimed with confidence that never before has the Jesus Prayer been practiced and loved as much as it is today."[8]

How to Pray the Jesus Prayer

In praying the Jesus Prayer one must avoid being mechanical, praying with vain repetitions (Matthew 6:7), or using it as a magic formula like a good luck charm. Instead, one must pray with inward sincerity and inward concentration. Aside from these general instructions each person must determine his or her form of praying the Jesus Prayer. According to Lev Gillet, a monk of the Eastern Church, "Every *repeated* invocation, in which the name of Jesus forms the core and motive force, is authentically the 'Jesus Prayer' in the Byzantine sense. One may say, for example, 'Jesus Christ' or 'Lord Jesus.' The oldest, the simplest, and in our opinion the easiest formula is the word 'Jesus' used alone."[9]

The Jesus prayer helps us deal with our distracting imaginations and thoughts. Bishop Ware points out that this is a positive and not a neutral or a negative spiritual strategy. Instead of "letting go" of the distractions in our minds, as we do in the Prayer of Rest and in Centering Prayer, we fill our minds with what is good.[10]

The challenge, of course, is to keep our minds on the meanings of the words and to address the prayer directly to the person of Jesus Christ, with conscious, active faith in him as Lord, Savior, Messiah, and Son of God. What helps is to coordinate the phrases in measured breathing, a tradition that goes back to the Eastern Fathers, namely, Climacus (7th century), who recommended that the remembrance of Jesus be united with our breathing. Hesychius (8th-9th century?) also urged that the Jesus Prayer be combined with our breathing. Similarly, Philotheus (9th-10th century?) urged that we not merely breathe air but God.[11] For these Eastern fathers, there was an immediate relationship between breathing in air and breathing in prayer.

Ignatius, also, practiced prayer with rhythmic breathing. He called it "A Measured Rhythmical Recitation," in which he recommended that a person with each breath express a single word or phrase of a prayer like "Our Father."[12]

You may want to try an expanded form of this prayer that includes the Prayer of Adoration and the Prayer of Rest along with rhythmic breathing. I would suggest the following combination of phrases.

"Lord Jesus Christ/I Adore You." While breathing in (or out — whatever works best for you), after you have slowed your breathing, say (inaudibly) with devotion, "Lord Jesus Christ." Then breathe out. As you breathe in the second time, say, "I adore you." Breathe out again. As you breathe in the third time, adore the Lord using the Attachment Insight on which you decided during your prayer period. Or adore him for who he is as the Divine Teacher, the suffering Servant, or the resurrected Lord. Or adore him by thinking of the image that you have of Jesus from the "Most Appealing" meditation. Repeat this for several additional breath cycles if you are finding it meaningful (a cycle is one breath in and out), or move directly to the next phrase.

"Son of God/I Rest in You." For the next phrase, breathe in, saying, "Son of God." Sense his presence within as you breathe out. As you breathe in again on the second cycle, think, "I rest in you." Consciously relax in his presence as you breathe out. As you breathe in for the third time, rest in the fact that you can completely trust him with your life and all your concerns. Or rest in the beauty of his creation ("by him all things were created" Colossians 1:16). Or rest in his wisdom, sovereignty, or some other attribute of God that relates to your Attachment Insight. As you rest, check to make sure that your hands and

other body parts are relaxed. Again, repeat this for several breath cycles or simply proceed to the next phrase.

"Have Mercy on Me/I Adore You." For the next phrase, as you breathe in say very consciously and intentionally, "Have mercy on me." As you breathe in on the second cycle, say, "I adore you." As you breathe for the third time, recognize the innumerable times that the Lord has had mercy on you. Adore him for the fact that he never ceases to have mercy upon you, that your life has been a good one because of his mercy, that out of his mercy he is giving you a greater desire to live his commandments, that today he will continue to show himself as a God of mercy, that in mercy he will give you direction, wisdom, or strength depending on what you need. Do this for several breath cycles or proceed immediately to the next phrase of the Jesus Prayer.

"I Am a Sinner/I Rest in Your Forgiveness and Love." For the final phrase, as you breathe in, say with compunction, "I am a sinner." As you breathe in the second time say, "I rest in your forgiveness and love." If, in fact, there is sin to confess, by all means confess it and forsake it as you continue for several more cycles of breathing. Your goal is to be able to rest in God's forgiveness and love, which is possible only if you also have forgiven others their trespasses against you (Matthew 6:12).

My preference is to move slowly from this form of active, discursive prayer to quietly abiding in Christ as I repeat the name of Jesus once every cycle of breath or once every two, three, or four cycles. The prayer becomes a quiet, loving, conscious communion with the person of Christ, an experience of the immediate presence of Jesus at a deeper level of consciousness. When distractions come, I may have to revert to the expanded form of the Jesus Prayer as described above or to the Jesus Prayer itself. But as soon as I am able to clear my mind of distractions, I return to the very special experience of being with Jesus without images, without discourse. I only speak the name "Jesus," and sense his presence within me or affirm his presence by faith alone.

During this time of quiet rest in the Lord, I sometimes experience a particular thought among other thoughts returning intermittently and leaving a distinct impression of something the Lord wants me to remember and enjoy or something he wants me to do or pray over. After I act upon the impression, I direct my attention in a loving way once again to Jesus.

The Benefits of the Jesus Prayer

What are some of the benefits of this prayer? The popular book, *"The Way of the Pilgrim,"* which first appeared in 1884, features an anonymous Pilgrim who practiced the "Jesus Prayer," which he also called the "Prayer of the Heart." Enraptured by the effect of the Jesus Prayer, the Pilgrim described on many occasions the way it impacted him:

> Sometimes I felt a sweet burning in my heart and such ease, freedom, and consolation that I seemed to be transformed and caught up in ecstasy. Sometimes I experienced a burning love toward Jesus Christ and all of God's creation. Sometimes I shed joyful tears in thanksgiving to God for His mercy to me, a great sinner. Sometimes difficult concepts became crystal clear and new ideas came to me which of myself I could not have imagined. Sometimes the warmth of the heart overflowed throughout my being and with tenderness I experienced God's presence within me.[13]

Sergei Hackel of the Russian Orthodox Church cautions that descriptions of delight such as the one just quoted should be a by-product of the prayer, not its end. Those who practice the prayer are to do so with simplicity and purity of intention. We should not seek to find pleasure or visions, but to be completely surrendered to the will of God.[14]

You may want to consider using the Jesus Prayer at the conclusion of your prayer period or integrating the Jesus Prayer with the Prayer of Adoration and the Prayer of Rest as I described above. My usual practice is to conclude my daily session of Devotional Prayer with 20 minutes of the Prayer of Rest.

In the moments that follow the Prayer of Rest, you may want to engage in prayer for others. The silence generated by the Prayer of Rest enables you to be more sensitive to the signals the Lord sends regarding the needs of others. The stillness also helps you maintain a purity of focus while praying for loved ones and friends.

SEVEN PRAYER EXERCISES

This week the prayer exercises include several memorable events in the life and teaching ministry of Jesus: *"The Calling of the First*

Disciples," "Sermon on the Mount," "Jesus Calms the Storm," and *"Jesus Sends Out the Twelve."* Also included is another of Ignatius' challenging thematic prayer exercises that I have adapted for our use. This one is called *"Three Types of Persons"*[15] and raises the all-important question of who really is the Lord of your life. The sixth prayer period is *"Repeat"* and invites us to return to any of the meditations in Week 1 through Week 4. The seventh is *"Review"* and provides opportunity to go back over the first six prayer exercises in Week 4.

The response recommendations in the first three prayer exercises are provided in considerable detail. In the exercises for days four and five, you will be given a chance to proceed on your own, without any coaching from me. If you aren't sure how to proceed, you can refer back to one of the first three prayer exercises.

Day One: "The Calling of the First Disciples"

Objective: Intimate knowledge of Christ that I might be *with* him, become *like* him, and live *for* him.

Scripture: Luke 5:1-11.

First point: Jesus taught the people from the boat.

Second point: Jesus guides Peter to a miraculous catch of fish.

Third point: The call of Jesus and the response of the disciples.

Your Response:

❖ Use Preparatory Prayer to ask God for help to achieve the objective of this prayer exercise. Example: "'Speak Lord, for your servant is listening' (1 Samuel 3:4). Help me to hear your still small voice. Give me intimate knowledge of Jesus, that I may know, love, and serve him more fully. I offer this prayer in his name. Amen."

❖ Using the Prayer of Imaginative Contemplation, visualize the three points listed above as you read the Gospel story. Come alive to the event. For example, in the first point, see Jesus getting into the boat as the people crowd to the shoreline to hear him. Imagine their clothing, their mingled voices, the freshness of the morning sea breeze, the sound of the boat creaking, the movement of light upon the water, the ripple of small waves lapping along the shore, the magnetism in Jesus' face, voice, and eyes as he looks at the people and teaches them.

✣ Next, step into the story and become part of the action. Join the disciples in the boat, putting out into deep water at the word of Jesus even though you had worked hard all night without catching anything. Grumble along with the fishermen. Feel some reluctance in letting down the nets. After all, a lot of time and effort was involved in retrieving and stacking them. Experience the astonishment and joy of the awesome catch. Notice the nets as they begin to break. Identify with Peter who knelt, expressing his unworthiness before one as great as Jesus. Imagine the expression and tone of Jesus' voice when he responded. Use your creative ability to pick up on further details of this marvelous story.

✣ Whenever your heart is warmed by the consideration of the character, words, or actions of Jesus, mark that portion of Scripture with an "A" denoting an Attachment Insight or jot down the thought or character trait for further consideration during your prayer exercise.

✣ It doesn't take much knowledge to fill and satisfy the soul. Seek to find one Attachment Insight (A) that you can grasp profoundly. Ask yourself, "What in the text moves me to want to attach myself to Jesus? What causes me to appreciate or love Jesus more?" That should lead to intimate knowledge of Jesus and delight in the Lord.

✣ If the Spirit is leading you to consider other truths or insights besides the attachment insights, by all means follow his lead. For instance, you may be struggling with the question of whether you want Jesus to have as much power and influence over you as he had over those first disciples. Take time to talk to him about your reservations. I am emphasizing Attachment Insights (A) in this meditation, but you may need to interact with the Spirit on other important issues.

✣ It is now time to turn to the Prayer of Adoration. Express praise to the Lord for who he is and give thanks for what he has done using your attachment insight to inspire devotion. Move next to the Prayer of Rest. Realize that your closest and best friend is within you. Humbly and gratefully enjoy his presence for several minutes. As your mind wanders, bring your thoughts back gently by returning to your attachment insight, or to your Motivating Statement, or to the objective of this exercise, or to the Jesus Prayer (*"Lord Jesus Christ, Son of God. Have mercy on me, a sinner"*). As soon as you can, move away from the images of the story to a sense of oneness with the living Christ who dwells within you. Relax in the awareness of the fact that the Lord loves you.

❖ After the Prayer of Rest and/or the Jesus Prayer, conclude your prayer exercise by thanking the Father for intimate knowledge of Christ that allowed you to be *with* Christ, gave you an increased desire to be *like* Christ, and motivated you to offer yourself in service *for* Christ. If you haven't already, take that final step and offer yourself *for* Christ.

❖ As you review your prayer exercise, you may want to continue the simple approach of asking yourself whether any of the activities you engaged in during this meditation hindered or helped achieve your objective in prayer. Or you may want to review your prayer exercise by using the more structured and comprehensive Prayer Response Sheet (see p. 67).

Day Two: "The Sermon on the Mount"

Objective: Intimate knowledge of Christ that I might be *with* him, become *like* him, and live *for* him.

Scripture: Matthew 5–7.

First point: The Beatitudes (Matthew 5:1-12).

Second point: The fulfillment of the law (Matthew 5:13-48).

Third point: The deception of praise and wealth (Matthew 6).

Fourth point: Positive relationships and warnings (Matthew 7).

Your Response:

A person new in prayer will generally cover a larger portion of Scripture during this prayer time. One who is mature in prayer and who has had a long acquaintance with the Scriptures can frequently fill an hour of prayer with only a small portion of Scripture. Thus, some of you may want to pray over all three chapters of the Sermon on the Mount. Others may prefer to limit themselves to Matthew 5 or a part of Matthew 5. Or you may want to concentrate on a portion of Matthew 6 or 7. Do not feel that you have to cover all four points above. Remember that it is not the completion of assignments that is important, but getting to know the person of Jesus and to experience the grace of his presence.

❖ Use a Preparatory Prayer to ask for God's help to achieve the objective of this prayer exercise.

❖ Use the Prayer of Consideration to search for at least one of each of the four types of insights. The Principle Insight (P) asks, "Is there a universal truth being expressed?" The Attachment Insight (A) asks, "What in the text causes me to admire, appreciate, love Christ more?" The Interior Insight (I) asks, "What in this text helps me to see and know myself as I really am?" The Detachment Insight (D) asks, "How can I deny myself and take up my cross?" The Prayer of Consideration uses an analytical approach, but we consider it prayer because we are deliberately bringing ourselves under the tutelage of the Holy Spirit and trying to stay sensitive to his direction as we seek insights. Remember that the Holy Spirit is your Spiritual Director and he desires to lead you according to your needs. Jesus promised, "He [the Holy Spirit] will guide you into all truth" (John 16:13-14).

❖ As you meditate on the insight that seems most relevant to you, offer a Prayer of Petition and ask God to help you become more like Jesus in some specific way.

❖ Assuming that you have been led to an insight that has given you intimate knowledge of Jesus, it is now time to turn to the Prayer of Adoration. Express your devotion to the Lord on the basis of the insight he has given you. Then, sit humbly and gratefully in communion with him for several minutes in the Prayer of Rest. When your mind wanders, bring it back gently by returning to your insight, or to your Motivating

Statement, or to the objective of the exercise, or to the Jesus Prayer. Keep in mind that your aim is a deeper sense of fellowship with Jesus.

✛ At the conclusion of your Prayer of Rest, offer yourself in service *for* Christ.

✛ Review your prayer period to determine what was helpful or detrimental.

Day Three: "Three Types of Persons"

Objective: To be free of attachment to a luxurious lifestyle or to anything that would hinder me from fulfilling God's will for my life.

Background: This meditation is designed to raise the question, "Who, after all, is the Lord of my life?" It involves three types of persons who acquired wealth and positions of authority, but not always with the best of motives. Nevertheless, these individuals desire to please God and to help others through their wealth and their positions of influence.

Scriptures: Matthew 21:28-32; Matthew 6:2-4; Matthew 6:31-34.

First point: The first type engages in talk but fails to take action.

Second point: The second type takes steps to help the poor, but does so to gain praise and recognition.

Third point: The third type desires Jesus to be Lord of all. This type is indifferent to wealth, or to any other attachment like a career or relationship that would interfere with following Christ. The third type can be counted on to hold on to wealth and other attractions or to release them depending on the guidance that God provides.

Your Response:

✛ Through Preparatory Prayer, ask God for the grace to be indifferent to wealth or any attachment that would hinder you from fulfilling God's will for your life.

✛ First type. Read Matthew 21:28-32 and note how the inaction of the second son illustrates the first type. He expressed willingness but failed to take action. Visualize a group of persons made up of the first type discussing the importance of knowing and loving God and helping those in need. Join the group by imaginatively placing yourself in it. Observe how all of you turn to other pursuits without following through on your intentions. Note that death comes to you before you do anything really decisive.

Express regret to God for procrastinating in this way, and ask (Prayer of Petition) the Lord to give you the grace to move from good intentions to action. If you are reminded of something you have been postponing, resolve to do it. Hold yourself accountable by asking a friend to call you once a week until you have fulfilled your intention.

✢ Second type. Read Matthew 6:2-4 and note how it illustrates the second type. Visualize a group of persons made up of the second type meeting together and place yourself in this group. Join the others as they write large checks to the church and to charities. All within the group are responsible and caring persons, but the giving is without sacrifice and the motive is for recognition and praise from others.

Express regret to God for giving in this manner in the past and ask the Lord to give you a generous and modest spirit, which gives in secret and looks only to God for reward.

✢ Third type. Read Matthew 6:31-34 and note how it challenges us to be like the third type. Visualize a group of persons made up of the third type and place yourself in it. With regard to money, you seek to give or not give according to the way in which the Lord guides you. You desire an inward freedom that liberates you from the love of money, the praise of men, career goals, relationships, or anything else that may hinder your ability to seek first the Kingdom of God and his righteousness.

Using the Prayer of Petition, ask the Lord to enable you to develop indifference toward all things, a willingness to keep or to give away depending on how God directs you.

✢ Conclude by reviewing the impressions God gave you as you considered the three points. Resolve to follow through on God's direction to rid yourself of any unhealthy or excessive material attachments or any other idols. Offer yourself to

God as his grateful and willing servant and tell him that you desire only what he wants you to do.

Day Four: "Jesus Calms the Storm"

Objective: Intimate knowledge of Christ that I might be *with* him, become *like* him, and live *for* him.

Scripture: Mark 4:35-41.

First point: Jesus announces his intention to cross the sea.   A storm comes.   Jesus sleeps.

Second point: Jesus' disciples question him.   Jesus is displeased with their lack of faith.

Third point: Jesus rebukes the elements.   They become calm.   The disciples marvel.

Your Response:

Try this prayer exercise without coaching from me.   Move through the prayer modes as you see fit.   Seek the direction of the Holy Spirit all the way through the review.   If you need help, review the response recommendations for Days One or Two.

Day Five: "Jesus Sends Out the Twelve"

Objective: Intimate knowledge of Christ that I might be *with* him, become *like* him, and live *for* him.

Scripture: Matthew 10:1-42.

First point: Christ gave them authority.

Second point: Christ taught them prudence and patience.

Third point: Christ told them how to go and what to preach.

Your Response:

Again,   try   this   prayer   exercise   without   coaching   from   me. Remember that the Holy Spirit is your Spiritual Director.

Day Six: "Repeat"

Use this *"Repeat"* prayer exercise to return to any of the exercises that you have had during the first four weeks. By developing greater competence in using the various prayer modes and in identifying the four types of insights ("P" "A" "I" "D"), you now have better skills and abilities for prayerful interaction with the Scripture. You may want to go back to an earlier meditation, like "Solace" (the Prodigal Son) in Week 1. Repeat it to see whether you receive more light with the new tools for meditation you are now able to use, and, more importantly, the greater sensitivity you have developed to the leading of the Holy Spirit.

Day Seven: "Review"

Review this week of exercises, looking for a unifying message that has repeated itself in several of the exercises.

FRIENDS ON THE JOURNEY

Bob — The downside to extra long prayer exercises

Bob was very disappointed in himself because he missed two days of prayer in a row. He was determined to get back on track and so he did three prayer exercises on the third day.

I assured him that there is no disadvantage in doubling or tripling the exercises or even having four or five meditations in one day. An eight-day Ignatian retreat usually contains four or five prayer exercises per day.

I asked how long he had prayed the day before he missed twice. He answered two hours. I pointed out that a long meditation of 90 minutes or more on any particular day often works against a 60-minute meditation the next day, even when the long meditation has been meaningful. For the sake of maintaining a daily prayer schedule, I suggested that his prayer periods be neither too long nor too short. Forty-five to 60 minutes is about right for Devotional Prayer, with 60 minutes preferable while you are going through this prayer program and learning new skills.

Cathy — A Christian leader who loves Attachment Insights

Cathy wondered whether it was really in her best interest to be focusing so much on attachment insights rather than seeking ways in which she could strengthen some of the deficiencies she saw in herself.

I told her of a retreat I once attended at the Prince of Peace Abbey in Oceanside, California. I spoke with Abbot Claude, then retired but who previously had been the abbot (superior) of that monastery for 30 years. I asked him whether the monks are cautioned against the tendency so many of us have of focusing too much on self-improvement rather than on the beauty of Christ.

His eyes sparkled as he affirmed in the most engaging way the absolute necessity of growing in love with Christ. He emphasized that we must draw constant inspiration from his life and words and example, and recognize that he is the living Christ who will transform us and enable us to grow in sanctification — but only as we keep our eyes fixed upon him.

This Christian leader was affirming in slightly different words what I have learned in working with many praying people: that the Attachment Insight (A), which invites us to delight in the greatness of Christ, is that which ultimately strengthens and transforms us.

I wasn't sure Cathy had been persuaded, but she nodded her head and said, "I think I can agree. I sense something positive happening when I come upon a special quality of Jesus and then pause to consider it, take some time to adore him for it, and then rest in his presence as I think about it."

WEEK 5

DEALING WITH DESOLATION

If you are like most participants in this prayer training, your experience with Devotional Prayer during the past few weeks has been very positive. However, along with the positive developments, you may have experienced an occasional sense of dryness and discouragement.

People seasoned in prayer expect intermittent periods of apathy and even feelings of separation from God. They know that the enemy of our souls seeks to weaken, disrupt, and, if possible, overthrow our trust in God. His customary strategy is to promote doubt and confusion. Instead of yielding to these disturbances, it is important for us to understand why we experience them and how you should respond.

Defining Desolation

When we discussed Heart Prayer in Week 2, we considered how emotions play a significant role in our prayer experience. We looked at Ignatius' description of consolations and saw that he described them as interior movements in the soul when we feel love for God. In addition to consolations, Ignatius indicated that we also experience confusion and agitation. Ignatius referred to these as desolation, which he described as follows:

> Darkness of soul, turmoil of spirit, inclination to what is low and earthly, restlessness rising from many disturbances and temptations which lead to want of faith, want of hope, want of love. The soul is wholly slothful, tepid, sad, and separated, as it were, from its Creator and Lord. For just as consolation is the opposite of desolation, so the thoughts that spring from consolation are the opposite of those that spring from desolation.[1]

God's people have always experienced disturbances and temptations that resulted in a sense of distance from God or sadness in prayer. This dryness is reflected in the hymns of the church. Isaac Watts describes it in *Come, Holy Spirit, Heavenly Dove*. The second stanza reads:

Dear Lord, and shall we ever live

99

At this poor, dying rate?
Our love so faint, so cold to Thee,
And Thine to us so great! (italics added)

George Croly's hymn, *Spirit of God, Descend upon My Heart*, contains in the second stanza similar expressions of a lack of spiritual perception.

I ask no dream, no prophet ecstasies,
No sudden rending of the veil of clay,
No angel visitant, no opening skies:
But take *the dimness of my soul* away. (italics added)

A confession of weakness and a want of love is found in the fourth stanza of John Newton's *How Sweet the Name of Jesus Sounds.*

Weak is the effort of my heart,
And cold my warmest thought,
But when I see Thee as Thou art,
I'll praise Thee as I ought. (italics added)

When Does Desolation Descend?

Desolation can come from a variety of conditions. First, a feeling of distance from God could be the result of an illness. A physical affliction will often have an adverse effect on devotions.

Second, a moral or spiritual lapse will result in desolation. A harsh and ugly exchange with a neighbor, a dishonest financial transaction, or an immoral sexual relationship will grieve the Holy Spirit. God will not be a partner to our sins. We must make things right, as David did when he came to God with a contrite heart and asked that his transgressions be blotted out (Psalm 51:9, 17). Only then will God restore the joy of our salvation.

Third, a want of faith and a want of hope may not be the result of a moral deviation, but of a psychological or emotional condition. It may be the result of the loss of a loved one, or the loss of a job, or simply boredom, or a mid-life crisis.

Or, fourth, we may feel discouraged, restless, and separated from God because earth is not heaven. We live in an imperfect world where things are not always fair. When evil prevails, prayer may become mechanical and God may seem distant.

These interruptions in our fellowship with God differ from what St. John of the Cross called the "dark night of the soul." A sixteenth century theologian and poet and one of the greatest spiritual directors in the church's history, St. John of the Cross had a special calling to guide men and women to total union with God through prayer in what he called the "dark night." The experience had nothing to do with moral failings or psychological obstacles, but rather with an advance in our familiarity with God. The expectation in his teaching, according to Thomas Green, was that we would experience deeper and longer silence from the Lord as we were drawn more closely to him.[2]

WHY GOD ALLOWS DESOLATION

Since desolation is experienced sooner or later by everyone who practices prayer, it is helpful to be aware of three major reasons why God allows us to experience these disturbances. This awareness will allow us to respond more intelligently to desolation. It may even enable us to welcome desolation since, in each of the three reasons, there are important benefits that can come to us from it.

Spiritual Correction

Perhaps the most common reason for desolation is that God uses it to correct us when we have sinned. The Bible is filled with examples of desolation coming upon those who have turned away from the commandments of the Lord. This was the case of the man in the Corinthian church who was to be handed "over to Satan," so that his sinful nature would be destroyed and his spirit saved on the day of the Lord (1 Corinthians 5:5). Cut off from other Christians, this man most likely experienced estrangement and loneliness and a want of hope and love. The practice of ostracism is sometimes referred to as "shunning" and facilitates the experience of desolation. It continues in some churches in our day and is a distinguishing mark of Amish life in America.

Christians are ripe for desolation when they get too chummy with the world, as this passage from the book of Revelation teaches: "You say, 'I am rich; I have acquired wealth and do not need a thing.' But you do not realize that you are wretched, pitiful, poor, blind and naked.... Those whom I love I rebuke and discipline. So be earnest, and repent" (Revelation 3:17, 19). Ignatius may have had God's rebuking and disciplining of such people in mind when he wrote: "First, we suffer desolation when it is our own fault because we have not lived our life of faith with any effort. We have become tepid and slothful and our very shallowness in the spiritual life has brought about the experience of desolation."[3]

It is the very rare person who has never been lethargic or superficial in living his or her faith. For example, Jesus repeatedly instructed us to pray, but many neglect to pray. As a result they become like the man Jesus spoke of in the closing paragraph of the Sermon on the Mount who heard the words of Jesus but did not do them. He is described as one who built his house upon sand. When the rains and flooding streams were joined with wailing winds and all three came against the structure, it collapsed (Matthew 7:24-27).

God permits these difficulties to get our attention. When our spiritual house comes crashing down around us, we realize that we must become serious about our discipleship to Jesus. Desolation should drive us to our knees to ask God if there might be some way in which we are ignoring, neglecting, or disobeying the words that Jesus has spoken to us. The good news is that if desolation has come to us because of sin, repentance will lift it.

Testing of Faith

A second reason that God allows desolation is that he uses it as a means of testing our faith. When dryness comes upon us, we would be wise to ask ourselves this question: "Will I be obedient to God's commandments even when I don't feel like doing them, even in the face of difficulties that shake my confidence in God's presence and protection?"

This matter of a test of faith became much more understandable to me as I was riding a bicycle on a South Carolina beach. It was a cool, lovely evening with the ocean at low tide, giving me a lot of room to maneuver the bike on the firm sand. As I glided along, I could hear the crackling of seashells beneath the wheels and the sound of the surf gently washing ashore. The mild ocean breeze on my face was refreshing. It was a delightful evening bike ride.

After a half-hour up the beach, I reversed direction to return to home base. A stiff, unyielding wind confronted me. I suddenly realized that the ride up the beach had been effortless because the wind had been at my back and had been boosting me along. To return, I had to lean into the strong breeze and pump against the wind. My legs ached by the time I got back to my starting point.

It dawned on me that this is how it is with consolation and desolation: consolation is the favorable wind behind us helping us along, while desolation is the afflicting wind in our face resisting our advance. When, for example, we attend an inspiring Bible conference or engage in Spirit-filled worship, consolations of joy and praise fill our hearts. During those times, it is easy to live the Christian life, to keep the commandments, to be gracious and forgiving toward others. That is because we are moving with the wind of the Spirit and it propels us forward to do God's will.

But when the wind is temporarily removed or, even worse, comes against us, we realize how much harder it is to live the life of an apprentice of Jesus. The resistant wind becomes a test of our staying power. It challenges us by raising the question: Will we remain on course in the face of problems as the Apostle Paul did *("I delight in weaknesses, in insults, in hardships, in persecutions, in difficulties."* [2 Corinthians 12:10])?

The analogy of the wise builder in Matthew 7:24-27 is again helpful. As disciples of Jesus, we construct our lives on the rock when we not only hear but also do what Jesus says. Even so, we are not shielded from rains, floods, or winds. Like everyone else, we experience storms that leave us in desolation. The storms damage the shutters, tear the roof, and flood the basement. We discover how weak we are in the face of such powerful forces. We realize that it is not within our power to overcome the storms or the dread that they bring. Nevertheless, we are expected to persevere when facing trials of many kinds (James 1:2).

In the midst of problems, our faith is tested in this way: Will we give in to grumbling, doubt, and vacillation? We are made máture and complete, not lacking anything, when we persist in faith and in that way pass the test (James 1:4).

Growth in Humility

God allows desolation, thirdly, to help us advance in humility. When desolation overwhelms us, we cannot arouse feelings of devotion for the Lord, or experience joy in singing songs of praise, or feel the warmth of love for Christians as we normally do. These are spiritual consolations that God from time to time granted us on other occasions but in times of desolation we realize anew that consolations are truly the gifts of God, that they cannot be attributed to ourselves. Seasons of desolation help us grow in our awareness that we are empty of fervor or devotion for God when left to ourselves (John 15:5b). That is humbling.

As a favorable wind pushes us along on a bicycle, just so, consolation pushes us along in the spiritual realm. While the wind is at our back, we cannot take credit for gliding with the wind. We know that it is not our pumping power that makes the ride effortless. Conversely, when the wind shifts and confronts us, as in the case of desolation in the spiritual realm, we realize that progress against the wind will be difficult. In this way, desolation leads us to an increase in humility, which means that we have an authentic grasp of who we are and what we can and cannot do. Humility counsels us to live as close to that truth as possible.

The tragic example of Peter's denial of Jesus is a case in point. The threat of arrest, the brutality of the Roman guards, and the possibility of death by crucifixion filled Peter with terror. The breeze that came from the comment of a servant girl had become a whirlwind that Peter could not manage despite the confidence he had expressed in himself when he said to Jesus, "Even if I have to die with you, I will never disown you" (Matthew 26:35). Peter ultimately made not one but three denials, as Jesus said he would: "Before the rooster crows, you will disown me three times." When Peter heard the rooster and remembered, he went outside and wept bitterly (Matthew 26:75). Shame, disgrace, and remorse descended upon Peter.

Peter had failed the test. His denial revealed to him how utterly deficient he was in himself and how very much he needed Jesus' strength. That increase in self-understanding was absolutely essential for Peter. It enabled him more than anything else to turn away from haughtiness and presumption and to grow in humility.

WHAT TO DO IN TIMES OF DESOLATION

How should we respond when we find ourselves experiencing darkness of soul or turmoil in our spirit? What is our best course of action when we feel separated from God?

Do Not Change Course

First, we must refuse *to reverse any decision made in prayer before we experienced desolation.* We must also avoid making any major, new decisions while struggling with desolation. The reason is that in desolation the evil spirit is attempting to obstruct God's will and direction for our lives. As we said in the section above, the Lord allows desolation to come to Christians to test them or to advance their growth in humility, but God is not the author of desolation.

For example, it was God's gentle leading to which we responded when we decided to enhance our habit of prayer. The enemy of our soul works against this decision by undermining our resolve and sending desolation. If we give in to desolation and quit praying, that would be tantamount to making the evil spirit our spiritual director, a mistake that would be laughable if it were not so destructive or common.

A friend of mine was pastor of a congregation when a highly regarded member of the church made false accusations against him. She accused him of sexual misconduct. He was deeply offended and troubled. At times, he experienced an absence of God. When he called a trusted mentor for counsel, he was told: "Pack your bags. You'll never survive that accusation, especially since it was made by a respected member of the church."

My friend wasn't sure that was good advice. Several years before, he had prayed about serving as pastor of that church and felt that he had received clear guidance from the Lord to accept the call. Having worked with me in this area of prayer, he knew that his decision, which had been made in consolation, should not be changed during a time of desolation. So, he decided to weather the storm. He stayed with the church. It took several years to resolve the problem, but his decision to stand firm enabled the church to discipline the person who had made false accusations and who, it was discovered, had harassed and manipulated several previous pastors.

Persevere in Prayer

When a period of dryness comes upon us, we will want to consider whether the dryness has come because of disorder in our lives or as an opportunity to mature in prayer. If the dryness is not a sign of spiritual or moral sickness, the Lord may be drawing us to a level of greater maturity in prayer, a maturity that requires faithfulness despite the heaviness of spirit or loss of interest that we may be experiencing. In this case, we *should do everything in our power to be patient and to persevere, to continue by remaining faithful even in this state of restlessness and sadness.* We must be determined to meet desolation head on. If we are tempted to pray less, we must pray more.

The model for perseverance in prayer during desolation is our Lord, himself. When he was in Gethsemane, we are told that he began to be "sorrowful and troubled" (Matthew 26:37). He took three of his disciples with him and said to them, "My soul is overwhelmed with sorrow to the point of death. Stay here and keep watch with me" (Matthew 26:38).

This is the first time in the Gospels that we find Jesus at this level of desolation. He coped with his anguish by asking friends to pray with him. After instructing them, Jesus went a short distance, fell with his face to the ground, and prayed *"My Father, if it is possible, may this cup be taken from me. Yet not as I will, but as you will"* (Matthew 26:39b).

When he rose from prayer and found his disciples sleeping, he challenged them to meet temptation head on through prayer: "Get up and pray so that you will not fall into temptation" (Luke 22:46).

When Jesus went away a second time he prayed, "Father if it is not possible for this cup to be taken away unless I drink it, may your will be done" (Matthew 26:42). He returned to his disciples hoping to find the support that friends can provide, but again he found them sleeping. So he left them and went away once more and prayed the third time, saying the same thing.

Not knowing the impenetrable will of God, Jesus in his human condition persevered in prayer and demonstrated a quality of submission and humility that must have pleased the heart of the Father. It is easy to be submissive when God communicates his will in an obvious manner with emotional assurances and a granting of power over temptation. But Jesus persevered in prayer when it seemed as though the Father had withdrawn every support and even reason itself. Thus, Jesus cried out on the cross, "My God, My God why have you forsaken me?" (Matthew 27:46b).

When we began this program, many of us were encouraged by consolations. The Lord was sensibly present to us and granted us a smooth journey with emotional favor and easy victory over temptation. He was moving us along, giving us an easy and delightful ride with the wind at our backs.

But, as we have indicated, the Lord's practice is occasionally to withdraw from our conscious experience. He is still very much with us since Jesus promised never to leave or to forsake us (Hebrews 13:5). However, we do not always "feel" his presence. The wind may even change directions and become a barrier of resistance. And yet, the one inflexible rule of spiritual direction is this: *We should never, for any reason whatever, neglect to pray.*

Know that Desolation Is Temporary

During the hours between the arrest and the crucifixion, we sense that Jesus was able to respond to the interrogations, physical abuse, and even his crucifixion with a serene and majestic dignity. Not until he uttered the words, "My God, my God, why have you forsaken me?" did desolation descend one final time to torment him. But death and desolation were overcome, finally, triumphantly, in the resurrection. Desolation was temporary for Jesus and is temporary most often for his followers as well.

What we must keep in mind is that the Spirit blows where he wills. Some people have engaged in Devotional Prayer for decades and have received encouraging consolations throughout their prayer history. They know all about dryness as spelled out by St. John of the Cross and they acknowledge that some Christians are granted a dark night experience. Yet, they are quick to remind themselves of Jesus' assurance that he intended his joy to be in them and that he wanted their joy to be complete (John 15:11). This emphasis on the fullness of joy was repeated by Jesus two more times in his final discourse and prayer (John 16:24; 17:13). It would therefore seem that joy, not dryness, should be the normative experience of Christmas.

Paul urged us to "rejoice in the Lord always," which presumes that joy in the Lord will be a continual possibility for us. He also promised that God's peace would guard our hearts and our minds in Christ Jesus (Philippians 4:4-7). These and other assurances seem to run counter to the idea that the only way one can become fully developed in prayer is to have an ongoing, ever-deepening dark night experience. There will be occasions of desolation, but under most circumstances we can expect them to be temporary.

SEVEN PRAYER EXERCISES

The prayer exercises this week consist of a series of episodes taken from the final year of Jesus' ministry: *"The Feeding of 5,000," "On Water," "Peter's Confession of Christ," "Transfiguration," "Mary-Martha."* Also included are a *"Repeat"* and a *"Review."*

By this time you may be developing a preference for one of the methods of Mental Prayer and may be tempted to use it exclusively. I would caution you against that. Instead, become as proficient as possible with each of the three mental prayer modes since each has its own special value. Later you will be able to shift from one to another, even in the midst of prayer sessions, depending on the Scripture you are considering. In the meantime, it will be to your advantage to become as expert as possible with each.

It is for this reason that I am recommending that you use Imaginative Contemplation with the meditation *"The Feeding of 5,000,"* Meditative Reading with the meditation *"On Water,"* and the Prayer of Consideration with the meditation *"Peter's Confession of Christ."* You will be free to select the prayer modes you prefer in the remaining prayer exercises.

Day One: "The Feeding of 5,000"

<u>Objective</u>: Intimate knowledge of Christ that I might be *with* him, become *like* him, and live *for* him.

108

Scripture: Matthew 14:13-21.

First point: The late hour; the disciples' request.

Second point: Christ fed the multitude.

Third point: The people had their fill; leftovers were taken up.

Your Response:

❖ Use Preparatory Prayer to ask for God's help in achieving the objective of this prayer exercise. The stanza of a hymn that relates to the exercise can be used as your preparatory prayer. The following is from the first stanza of *Break Thou the Bread of Life*:

> Break thou the bread of life, dear Lord to me,
> as thou didst break the loaves beside the sea;
> beyond the sacred page I seek thee, Lord;
> my spirit pants for thee, O living Word. Amen.

❖ Using Imaginative Contemplation, visualize the three points listed above, each in its turn, carefully reading the Scripture passage to include all of the details. Come alive to the sights, sounds, smells and feelings of the event.

Step into the story so that you become part of the action. Sense the excitement of the families as they sit in circles on the grass wondering what is going to happen. Watch Jesus as he prays to the Father, breaks the loaves, and gives the bread and the fish to each of the disciples. Notice the amazement of the disciples as they distribute the food and discover bread and fish replaced as quickly as they distribute what they have. Sit in one of the circles, taste the bread and the fish, enter into the astonishment of the people as they talk about the miracle. See the compassion Jesus has for the people. Let him look into your eyes as though you were there on that day. Feel the love that he has for you now.

❖ Instead of two or three Attachment Insights (A), seek to find one that you can grasp profoundly. Ask yourself, "What in the text moves me to want to attach myself to Christ? What causes me to appreciate or love Christ more?" Try to understand why he takes the actions and says the words that he does. Seek intimate knowledge of Christ.

✢ Be conscious of any consolations that you may feel during the prayer period (peace, joy, praise, urge for self-giving). If you are experiencing Heart Prayer, stay with it as long as it lasts. Recognize it as a gift from the Lord and thank him.

✢ If you are led to consider other insights besides the Attachment Insights (A), feel free to go with them.

✢ Assuming that you have been led to an Attachment Insight (A) that has given you intimate knowledge of Christ and that you consequently feel a deep love for him, offer a Prayer of Adoration to the Lord.

✢ Using the Prayer of Petition, you may want to ask the Lord to multiply your resources in an area of your life that needs his help. Offer him your five loaves and two fish, and then give yourself in service *for* Christ. Seek to do this in a way that comes from the depths of your heart. Repeat your offering several times.

✢ Continue by sitting humbly and gratefully in his presence in the Prayer of Rest for several minutes. Do not be surprised or disappointed if your mind wanders. Return to your Attachment Insight (A), or to your Motivating Statement, or to the objective of the prayer exercise, or to the Jesus Prayer. Remember, your overall aim is to commune with Christ; that is, to be in a state of intimate, heightened sensitivity and receptivity to him.

✢ Review your prayer exercise by asking yourself whether any of the activities in which you engaged during this meditation hindered or helped you in achieving the objective of this prayer exercise. Or, use the more structured "Prayer Response Sheet" (p. 67) for review questions.

Day Two: *"On Water"*

Objective: Intimate knowledge of Christ that I might be *with* him, become *like* him, and live *for* him.

Scripture: Matthew 14:22-36.

First point: Christ dismissed the crowds and prayed alone.

Second point: Christ walked upon water.

Third point: Christ saved and reprimanded Peter. The wind ceased.

Your Response:

- ✦ Ask for the Lord's help in achieving the objective of this prayer exercise.

- ✦ Use Meditative Reading as you pray over Matthew 14:22-36. Read the text out loud giving emphasis to important words or phrases. Consider the first point as thoroughly as you can. Then move on to the second point, and then to the third. Remember, in meditative reading you approach the text with patient humility, waiting for words, phrases, and ideas to make their impact on you as you read and reread the text.

  During the reading of the passage, carry on a conversation with the Lord. Interact with him after each verse or two. Tell him what you notice. Invite him to give you understanding. Pause to listen for a response from him. This often comes in the form of an insight that touches both mind and heart. As you are impressed with words or thoughts, weigh their significance. Stay with and experience, as fully as you can, the positive emotions they evoke. Respond to their inspiration and challenge.

- ✦ After you have savored a word or idea that the Lord has drawn to your attention, consider what type of insight it might be: Principle (P), Attachment (A), Interior (I), or Detachment (D). Remember that with Meditative Reading, you do not search for insights. Instead, you allow yourself first to be impressed by the words of Scripture. After you focus on a certain thought or word, then you may want to process that thought further by considering the type of insight it might be. This differs from the way in which you proceed with the Prayer of Consideration. With it, you move into the Scripture intentionally searching for specific insights.

- ✦ After you have offered praise to the Lord through the Prayer of Adoration, humbly and gratefully enter into the Prayer of

Rest. Whenever your mind begins to wander, bring it back by returning to your Attachment Insight (A), your Motivating Statement, or the Jesus Prayer. Keep in mind that your objective at this point is to be *with* Christ, to experience communion *with* the Lord.

✚ As you review your prayer period, consider how well you achieved the objective of the prayer exercise. Did you experience intimate knowledge of Christ? Were you *with* Christ during the exercise and *with* him in a more intentional way during the Prayer of Rest? Did you have a desire within you to become more *like* Christ? Did you offer a Prayer of Petition asking the Lord to make you more like Christ? Did you conclude your session by giving yourself in service *for* the Lord? If not, take a moment to do that: offer yourself as a living sacrifice, holy and pleasing to God — this is a spiritual act of worship (Romans 12:1-2).

Day Three: "Peter's Confession of Christ"

Objective: Intimate knowledge of Christ that I might be *with* him, become *like* him, and live *for* him.

Scripture: Matthew 16:13-27.

First point: Peter confesses Jesus as the Christ.

Second point: Jesus predicts his sufferings and coming glory.

Third point: Jesus describes the conditions of discipleship.

Your Response:

✚ Through Preparatory Prayer, ask the Lord to help you achieve the objective of this prayer exercise.

✚ Use the Prayer of Consideration to work though Matthew 16:13-27. Read through the material looking for one or more of each of the four types of insights: Principle (P), Attachment (A), Interior (I), and Detachment (D). Begin with Attachment Insights (A): "What in the text causes me to appreciate and love Christ more?" Which Attachment

Insight stands out in your thought as the most impressive or appealing?

❖ Next consider Principle Insights (P). There are several extremely important Principle Insights (P) in this passage. Ask yourself, "Is there a fundamental truth being expressed in this passage?"

❖ Identify any Interior Insights (I) that might help you gain an increase in self awareness. Ask, "What in this text helps me see and know myself as I really am?"

❖ The conditions for discipleship set forth by Jesus provide several important Detachment Insights (D). Note at least one. Consider, "How does this text instruct me to deny myself and to take up my cross?"

❖ Talk to the Lord about which of these insights he wants you to dwell upon most deeply. If none is drawing you, go with an Attachment Insight.

❖ Take time to praise the Lord with the Prayer of Adoration, and then remain humbly and gratefully in the presence of the Lord in the Prayer of Rest. If your mind wanders, nudge it to return to your Attachment Insight (A) or other type of insight, noting that the Lord is the author of every helpful insight. Or, go to your Motivating Statement or to the Jesus Prayer.

❖ I find it helpful to thank the Lord for enabling me to achieve the objective of the exercise by offering a few words of prayer with each breath cycle. Breathing slowly, I say inaudibly as I breathe in (or out, depending on what works best for you), "Thank you — for intimate knowledge — of yourself — that I might be *with* you — become *like* you — and live *for* you." I may do this three or four times then move to a more passive Prayer of Rest, simply resting in the presence of the Lord, whispering the name "Jesus" from time to time to heighten my sensitivity toward the Lord when distracted by thoughts. The mechanics of rhythmic breathing are secondary. Getting the mind to focus on the immediate presence of the Lord is the goal. Expressing the words with each breath helps to focus the mind.

❖ As you review your prayer exercise, ask yourself, "Was I sensitive to Heart Prayer? Did I give thanks for it?"

Day Four: "Transfiguration"

<u>Objective</u>: Intimate knowledge of Christ that I might be *with* him, become *like* him, and live *for* him.

<u>Scripture</u>: Matthew 17:1-9.

<u>First point</u>: The three disciples; Jesus transfigured.

<u>Second point</u>: Jesus spoke with Moses and Elijah.

<u>Third point</u>: The voice from heaven; Jesus' reassurance.

Your Response:

Proceed as the Holy Spirit leads you. Ask the Spirit for guidance and try to follow any impressions that you think may be coming from the Spirit. The "Your Response" comments in the first three meditations above were provided in considerable detail in case you felt a need to refer to them in this and the remaining prayer exercises.

Day Five: "Mary-Martha"

<u>Objective</u>: Intimate knowledge of Christ that I might be *with* him, become *like* him, and live *for* him.

<u>Scripture</u>: Luke 10:38-42.

<u>First point</u>: Jesus and his disciples were guests at the home of Martha.

<u>Second point</u>: Mary sat at the Lord's feet listening to him. Martha complained.

<u>Third point</u>: Jesus responded.

Your Response:

This is a wonderful story about the priority of being *with* Christ. Proceed as the Spirit leads you.

Days Six and Seven: "Repeat" and "Review"

Repeat and review as you are led by the Spirit.

FRIENDS ON THE JOURNEY

Bob — God's Word is utterly personal for you!

Bob had a great week with the prayer exercises and found the stories coming alive through his use of Imaginative Contemplation. Indeed, the stories became so real, the consolations so rich, and the insights so inspiring that he could hardly wait to share them with the Sunday school class he teaches. By the end of the week, he was spending more time in his devotions thinking about insights that would help members of his adult Sunday school class than on what the Bible passage had to say to him. As a result, his personal communion with Christ began to slip. When we got together, he asked about this.

I pointed out to Bob that his problem was common among pastors and Sunday school teachers. Each week they have to come up with stimulating sermon or lesson material. As they turn to the Bible for their personal devotions, their thoughts inevitably turn to the people they serve. Unless they fight this tendency, they lose out on their personal time *with* Christ. Their concern for their parishioners or students is admirable, but, in the long run, their ministry will suffer.

Years ago, I was impressed with a paragraph by Dietrich Bonhoeffer that addressed this issue. I shared his advice with Bob:

> In our meditation we ponder the chosen text on the strength of the promise that it has something utterly personal to say to us for this day and for our Christian life.... We do not ask what this text has to say to other people. For the preacher this means that he will not ask how he is going to preach or teach on this text, but what it is saying quite directly to him. It is true that to do this we must first have understood the content of the verse, but here we are not expounding it or preparing a sermon or conducting Bible study of any kind; we are rather waiting for God's Word to us.[4]

Cathy — Extending the Prayer of Rest to ten minutes

Cathy felt that she was making good progress in all areas of Devotional Prayer except for the Prayer of Rest. She was able to experience quiet for two or three minutes, but felt overwhelmed by the suggestion that she extend her time to ten minutes. She asked for suggestions.

I went over once again the method I frequently use during the final segment of my prayer period. I covered it in Week 4, but have found that it needs repetition and reinforcement before most individuals will try it or make it a part of their own prayer experience.

Having meditated on a passage of Scripture, I sit in a lounge chair with hands folded and begin with the first phrase of the Jesus Prayer: "Lord Jesus Christ." I say this inaudibly, slowly, and reverently as I breathe out. As I breathe out a second time, I say, "I adore you." In doing this, I am speaking to the living Christ who is present within me. My intention is to tell Jesus I admire and am committed to him. My thoughts are generally related to one of the Attachment Insights I received during the prayer exercise. For example, in the *"The Feeding of 5,000"* (Matthew 14:14) I might say, "I adore you for having compassion on the people." I slow my breathing so that I am very deliberate in my words and thoughts. I frequently repeat the three-fold cycle: the name, "Lord Jesus Christ," the statement of adoration, "I adore you!" and the Attachment Insight, "I adore you for having compassion on the people." I may do this for a total of nine breathe cycles, if that helps me keep my mind on Jesus and on my expression of adoration.

I indicated to Cathy that some people wonder whether this might be considered "vain repetition." I explained that I did not think it was since the words are not spoken in a mechanical way without meaning. I am not babbling or engaged in a mechanical technique, nor am I seeking or mental inactivity. I am addressing the person of Jesus with sincerity and concentration. As for repetition, Jesus surely did not prohibit that since in Gethsemane he went away and "prayed the third time, saying the same thing" (Matthew 26:44).

Then I breathe out and say, "Son of God." I follow that during the second breathe cycle with the phrase, "I rest in you." The thought that usually runs through my mind during the third breathe cycle is the major attachment insight I received during the prayer period. It is usually related to some aspect of Jesus' love, wisdom, or power, and I simply rest in the security of his greatness. In the feeding of the 5,000, I might say, "I rest in your power to multiply five loaves and two fish into enough food to feed thousands" (Matthew 14:20). Again, I may repeat this entire process two or three times. As I say, "I rest in you," I notice whether my hands, face, and other parts of my body have entered into a restful state, free from tension.

Next, I say, "Have mercy on me," and I follow that breathe cycle with, "I adore you." Then, during the third breathe cycle, the thought that often comes to my mind is that I adore him for extending his mercy to me in countless ways throughout my life.

Next, I say, "I am a sinner." I conclude by saying, "I rest in your love and forgiveness." I also often close with the final petition of the Lord's Prayer, "Deliver me from evil," saying it with emphasis for several cycles.

I find it helpful to follow each phrase of the Jesus Prayer with the words, "I adore you," or "I rest in you." Usually the first and third phrases are followed by "I adore you," and the second and fourth are followed by "I rest in you."

I may go through this entire process two or three times until my mind is focused and I can move into a more passive, restful communion with the Lord. When I reach that point, I shift from offering these words to a quiet and reverent mention of the name of Jesus once every cycle or every other cycle of breath, while sensing his immediate presence within me or simply affirming his presence by faith. I open myself up to his love to the best of my ability, allowing myself to be loved by him. This final stage of passive communion with the Lord is the highlight of my daily experience of Devotional Prayer. During this time, I am in a special sense enjoying intimate fellowship with Christ, abiding in Jesus, communing with the individual, living, acting, and holy God of Christian theology, and not merely with a pantheistic, impersonal life force that supposedly exists in everything but does nothing and demands nothing.

I concluded my comments by suggesting to Cathy that she avoid two opposite tendencies—one of being the slave of methods and the other of despising them. The ideas I shared with her would be useful only if she derived profit from them. If after trying to pray according to my suggestions she did not experience interior devotion, she should feel free to set my suggestions aside or to modify them in a way that would be more profitable for her.

WEEK 6
FINDING GOD'S WILL FOR YOU

When faced with a decision that will affect our lives in a major way, we instinctively turn to God for guidance. Sometimes he directs us with crystal clarity. But often, he does not. And we are left wondering how to discern God's will, if not with certainty, at least with reasonable confidence.

I know of no more effective means of finding God's will than the counsel provided by Ignatius. He calls his guidelines *Three Times When a Correct and Good Choice of a Way of Life May Be Made.*[1] I have shared Ignatius' advice with a variety of people and the guidelines have proven to be invaluable time and again. Yet I have spoken of the process discreetly. It presupposes a serious commitment to God, detachment from greed, glory, and power, and an ability to use some of the methods of prayer taught in this eight-week program.

GUIDELINES FOR FINDING THE WILL OF GOD

When the will of God is not explicitly revealed to us in the Bible, we can, with varying degrees of certainty, discover it under the following circumstances.

1. *Knowing God's Will with Certainty*

First, we can know the will of God for ourselves with complete confidence when God discloses his will to us conspicuously so that we know without doubt what God wants us to do. The conversion of Paul is an illustration of this type of a divine disclosure:

> As he neared Damascus on his journey, suddenly a light from heaven flashed around him. He fell to the ground and heard a voice say to him, "Saul, Saul, why do you persecute me?"
>
> "Who are you, Lord?" Saul asked.

"I am Jesus, whom you are persecuting," he replied. Now get up and go into the city, and you will be told what you must do." (Acts 9:3-6)

As a result of this experience with God, Paul knew who was speaking to him and what he had to do. He immediately departed for Damascus, feeling certain that this was God's holy will for him.

2. Knowing God's Will with a High Degree of Confidence

A second way of knowing God's will, not with the certainty described in the previous subsection but with a high degree of confidence, is when we experience strong negative feelings or strong positive feelings toward a choice. Let's begin with negative feelings.

When experiencing strong negative feelings. When we experience turmoil, anxiety, sadness, discouragement, frustration, temptation, restlessness, loss of faith, hope, and love, or a sense of the absence of God, we are in desolation. During these times, as explained in Week 5, we know that we should not make major decisions. Nor should we change decisions made prayerfully at an earlier time. This is because desolation is not God's voice for the faithful Christian. As Scripture indicates: "When tempted no one should say, 'God is tempting me.' For God cannot be tempted by evil, nor does he tempt anyone" (James 1:13).

Temptation comes from Satan. Through continual deceptions, he raises doubts and anxieties about God's love, or tempts us to grumble and complain about our circumstances and to withdraw from the ministry to which God has called us.

I have known several pastors who felt compelled to resign from their positions following stormy congregational business meetings. In each case, power groups came against them. At one of the churches, the integrity and motives of the pastor were called into question. The pastor was deeply hurt, felt he no longer could lead the congregation, and resigned on the spot. In another church, a pastor whose judgment and leadership were being challenged by a sizable minority felt such a letdown that he "threw in the towel," as he put it, and informed his congregation that he would not continue as pastor.

The critical mistake of both of these men was to make a career-changing decision while they were experiencing turmoil and desolation. A second critical mistake was to reverse — while experiencing desolation — the decisions they had made in prayer several years before to serve their respective congregations. Both pastors should have waited until desolation had lifted. (Remember, desolation is temporary.) When we are angry, defensive, resentful, or vindictive, discerning the Spirit's still, small voice is extremely difficult.

When experiencing strong positive feelings. In contrast to the way of Satan, God gives us consolation to guide us along the way of godliness. He provides hope and encouragement to keep us in his path as he did when he appeared to Paul and said, "Take courage! As you have testified about me in Jerusalem, so you must also testify in Rome" (Acts 23:11). Thus, if we are considering a choice that we think is the will of God for us and we experience an increase in enthusiasm, joy, and peace, we can assume that the Lord most likely has granted the consolations.

I say "most likely" because, unfortunately, the devil can just as easily switch from desolation to consolation. "Satan himself masquerades as an angel of light" (2 Corinthians 11:14). When the enemy gives strong positive feelings, however, it is for the purpose of drawing us away from God, of getting our attention on lesser things.

For this reason it is of utmost importance to discern the source of these positive feelings. Ignatius recommended that we do this by examining the beginning and middle and end of the course of our thoughts. If they are good and directed to what is entirely right, we have assurance that the positive feelings are from the Holy Spirit. But thoughts that at first seem right and good may terminate in something evil, or distracting, or less good than expected. Or they may end in what weakens us, or gives us less freedom to follow God's will, and in that way destroys the peace and tranquility which we had before. That would indicate that the consolations had come from an evil source. To sum up, when dealing with positive feelings one must be convinced that the consolations do not arise from, continue in, or terminate in something harmful, but rather arise from, continue in, and terminate in that which is good and entirely right.[2]

Good feelings without a preceding cause. One way we can be assured of correct decision-making is when we have strong positive feelings without a preceding cause. That is because, according to Ignatius, only God can give consolation to a person without any previous reason.[3] Thomas Green defined a preceding cause as "some reflection in the understanding, some image in the imagination, some activity of the senses, which leads us to a sense of joy, peace or consolation."[4] Prior activity in the senses or the faculties would indicate that the consolation has a preceding cause.

What would be an example of good feelings without a preceding cause? The Lord could give positive feelings to a person about to have radical surgery for cancer even if this person had not been encouraged by a friend, or was not buoyed by a promise from Scripture, but was simply facing the grim prospect of this operation. If suddenly this individual were filled with the tenderness and peace of the Lord, that would be an instance of consolation without preceding cause.

Or, in the case of a person making a choice, suppose someone was in a Christian ministry in which funding had dropped or disappeared. Reason would advise that person to leave that ministry and find another job. But what if that person continued to experience an extraordinary sense of peace to continue in his ministry despite economic duress? That could be consolation without preceding cause.

3. Finding God's Will with Confidence — 12-Day Process

There is a third way to discern the Lord's will with confidence, though not with the certainty or high degree of confidence described in the preceding subsections. This can occur even when we are facing a major decision in life but do not have clear feelings or convincing reasons to choose one option over the other. The pros and cons for either choice seem to balance one another.

Preparations. In this situation, we discern the Lord's will through a 12-day prayer process in which we examine our feelings of consolation even though they may be slight. The process is slow but can lead to a firm assurance of God's will. We proceed as follows.

(1) *Recommit to the goal of your life.* Sitting comfortably before the Lord, remind yourself of your "Basic Want" (Week 1, Day One) or the goal of your life. Your decision in the matter before you should enable you to contribute to your life goal, whether that goal is "to seek first the kingdom of God and his righteousness" (Matthew 6:33); or to adore God; or to love, honor, and reverence God; or to "make disciples of all nations" (Matthew 28:19); or to live the Sermon on the Mount; or "to glorify God, and to enjoy him forever;"[5] or some other life goal.

(2) *Focus on the two choices.* With as much clarity as possible, place before your mind the two choices between which you need to decide. Let's suppose that the two choices are to accept a new career job offer or to stay where you are. Either option would have to be an ethical choice, one that would honor God and be in harmony with his Word. An unethical option like getting even with your enemy by punishing him would evoke anxiety and restlessness; the Spirit would bring turbulence to a Christian over a choice that is morally questionable.

(3) *Seek impartiality.* Imagine a balance at equilibrium; that is the kind of disinterest you are to seek. Your goal is to be as easily influenced to go to the right as to the left, to take the thing proposed as to leave it, or to leave it as to take it, depending upon how the Lord moves you. This lack of bias requires detachment and provides the freedom to choose God's will. This is why detachment is an essential precondition to discernment. How does one acquire this detachment? The four meditations — *"Most Appealing"* (Week 2), *"Two Banners"* (Week 3), *"Three Types of Persons"* (Week 4), and especially *"Four Degrees of Humility"* (Week 6) — are designed to improve one's capacity for detachment. A high degree of detachment makes discernment possible. Without detachment, discernment is improbable.

To reach a more complete state of impartiality, you may want to sing softly and devotionally one or two of the following hymns of commitment and submission: *"Have Thine Own Way, Lord!" "I Will Serve Thee," "Rise Up, O Men of God," "O Love That Will Not Let Me Go," "Lead Me to Calvary," "I Surrender All," "Am I a Soldier of the Cross?" "Father, I Adore You."* Also, pray the Prayer of Rest for ten minutes.

(4) *Engage in Preparatory Prayer.* Using Preparatory Prayer, ask the Lord to guide you into that choice which best enables you to fulfill the goal of your life.

Twelve Days of Discernment. The discernment takes 12 days, six days of discernment and six days of confirmation. If there is a consistent discernment during the first six days, it may not be necessary to engage in the full six days of confirmation. For purposes of illustration, we will assume that you are seeking direction from the Lord regarding whether you should accept a new career opportunity being offered to you or stay in the job you currently have.

First Day

(1) Compare pros and cons. On this first day, you assume that the Lord wants you to step out and take the new position. List the advantages and disadvantages of taking the new career. Take into consideration the consultations you have had with your loved ones, close Christian friends, or your small group, weighing all the while the goal of your life and rejecting selfish or sensual motives. After you have considered and compared the advantages and disadvantages of accepting this new career, put your list away and move from the thinking level to the feeling level. This is explained in the next two steps.

(2) Request confirmation. Indicate to the Lord that you have assumed for purposes of this prayer time that he wants you to accept the new career opportunity. Using the Prayer of Petition, request the Lord to confirm that decision with peace if that truly is his will for you.

(3) Sit quietly before the Lord in prayer and be sensitive to the emotions you experience. Your goal is to be as sensitive as you can to feelings of peace, joy, calmness, serenity, confidence, disturbance, confusion, frustration, or caution. Remember that it is your feelings that you discern. Others can come up with the list of advantages and disadvantages, but the way you feel about this option is unique to yourself. Positive emotions such as peace are an indication that this could be God's will for you.

(4) Record impressions. Enter your discernment in a spiral notebook or your journal and indicate what you felt. *It will be important to record your feelings each day so that you can have a record of your*

prayer experience. Thank the Lord for the directions you received, whether you received peace or you didn't. Conclude by offering yourself to God and to his service.

Second Day

Repeat with alternative choice. The second day is a repeat of all the steps taken in the first day except that you assume that the Lord wants you to take the alternative choice, which in this case would be to stay in the position that you currently hold. Thus, after making the four preparations for prayer, (1) recommit to the goal of your life, (2) focus on the two choices, (3) seek impartiality, and (4) engage in Preparatory Prayer, proceed with the four steps of discernment described above. They are (1) compare pros and cons, (2) request confirmation, (3) be sensitive to the emotions you experience, and (4) record impressions.

You will want to gauge the extent to which one option or the other provides a positive emotional response. At the same time, recognize that you may not come up with an entirely consistent response. That's because your time in prayer may be distracted on a particular day by noise, illness, or even something as insignificant as a digestive problem. Or, you may not yet be skillful in sensing the inward movement of the Spirit. These and other factors affect the accuracy with which you discern your feelings. This is why it is important to extend the discernment process beyond one, two, or three days. By praying 12 days, you will have taken enough time to test for consistency of response.

Third Day

(1) Advise an imaginary individual faced with the same choices. As you prepare to enter into prayer for guidance on the third day, go through the same preparatory steps: (1) recommit to the goal of your life, (2) focus on the two choices, (3) seek impartiality, and (4) engage in Preparatory Prayer. You are not ready to proceed until you have taken these actions.

Next, imagine a faithful Christian who wants your help in his or her attempt to respond fully to God's will. You have never met before, but your heart goes out to him or her in such a way that you truly want the very best for this person. Without trying to control or manipulate, advise him or her as persuasively as you can to accept the new career position being offered. After you have gone through this role-playing, consider how you expressed yourself. Analyze the reasons you gave. Reflect on how you felt as you sought to influence this person.

(2) Request confirmation. If your advice for the stranger was the advice the Lord wants you to give to yourself, ask the Lord for validation. Monitor your feelings.

(3) Compare the feelings you had the first two days with those on the third. Thank the Lord for the results, whether positive or negative. Give yourself to him and to his service.

Fourth Day

The fourth day is a repeat of all the steps taken in the third day except that you assume that the Lord wants you to persuade the imaginary person to stay in the position that he or she currently holds.

Fifth Day

(1) View the results of your decision as though you were looking back at it at your moment of death. Once again, prepare yourself for guidance by making the four preparations for prayer. When ready to proceed, imagine seeing yourself in bed just before death. Assume that you had chosen to take the new career employment that is being offered to you and that you are looking back at that decision made 10, 30, or 50 years before. Try to imagine some of the results of that decision. Can you endorse that decision from the vantage point of your moment of death? Can you feel peaceful about it?

(2) Request confirmation. Ask the Lord to confirm the rightness of that decision that would have been made years before by giving you his peace. Be as sensitive as you can to the emotions that you experience.

(3) Record your impressions and give thanks to God. Compare the feelings you had the first four days with the fifth. Thank the Lord for the indications you are receiving, whether positive or negative, and offer yourself to him and to his service.

Sixth Day

Do the same thing that you did in the Fifth Day, except assume that you decided to stay in your current position and you are looking back from your deathbed on that decision.

Seventh through Twelfth Day – Confirmation

By this point in the process, you should be able to see a pattern of consistency or inconsistency. *If the pattern is inconsistency, confusion, and frustration, it is not appropriate to move ahead with a decision.* You may want, instead, to schedule a follow-up discernment at a later time. If a decision needs to be made because of time considerations, I would advise against accepting the job offer. As indicated earlier in the chapter, we should not change decisions in the midst of confusion and frustration. If, however, the pattern is consistent or relatively consistent in favor of one of the choices, I recommend an additional six days of discernment, asking God to confirm the decision to which you think he has led you.

Let's assume that you have relative peace about accepting the new career opportunity. You proceed on days seven, nine, and eleven by repeating the discernment sessions from days one, three, and five, asking God to confirm this choice. The prayer at each session would be along these lines: "Lord, I believe that you are leading me to decide in favor of accepting the new career position. If this is the case, please confirm this as your direction for me by giving me your peace."

On alternative days, repeat days two, four, and six, but assume that the Lord does not want you to stay at your present job. The prayer at each session would be along these lines: "Lord, I believe that you are leading me to decide against staying in my present position, and that, instead, you want me to accept the new career position. If this is the case, please confirm this as your direction for me by giving me your peace."

I have followed this procedure for almost all of the major decisions I have made during the past 20 years. Each time, the Lord has given me fairly consistent peace on one or the other of the two options. Several times I have been surprised by receiving peace over an option which I initially thought would be ruled out. The other option seemed more in accord with God's will for me or had more positive reasons in support of it. Yet, on several occasions I have received peace in support of what at first appeared to be the less desirable option.

I might add that I have never been disappointed with any of the decisions I have made using these guidelines. When doubts have assailed me and I have had occasion to look back and wonder whether I had made a correct decision, the process has provided reassurance time and again.

The diligence involved in devoting 12 days, usually one hour per day, in seeking the will of God gives assurance that you have given yourself every opportunity to be led by God. It is also a demonstration of your desire to honor God. On the Day of Judgment, a demanding process like this would perhaps allow one to say, "Lord I truly wanted to know and follow your will. As you know, I opened myself up as best I could to discern your will for my life in that matter."

SEVEN PRAYER EXERCISES

The Prayer Exercises feature four incidents that took place at the end of the public ministry of Jesus: *"Lazarus," "Jesus Anointed," "Palm Sunday,"* and *"Jesus Cleanses the Temple."* Following these Gospel meditations is Ignatius' thematic exercise, *"Four Degrees of Humility."*[6] Many consider this meditation the high point of the *Spiritual Exercises*. Its underlying issue is to raise the question of whether we are willing to be totally influenced by Jesus Christ. A *"Repeat"* session allows us to go back over any prayer exercise in Parts I or II. A *"Review"* exercise invites us to consider Week 6 as a whole.

Day One: *"Lazarus"*

Objective: Intimate knowledge of Christ that I might be *with* him, become *like* him, and live *for* him.

Scripture: John 11:1-45.

First point: Mary and Martha inform Jesus of the sickness of Lazarus.

Second point: Jesus claims to be the Resurrection and the Life.

Third point: Jesus raises Lazarus by a command, "Lazarus, come out!"

Your Response:

✠ Ask for the Lord's help to achieve the objective of this prayer exercise. Example: "Dear Lord, I desire to increase my devotion to you. Help me to take attention off myself and focus on you. Help me to see your glory in this story. I want to love you with all my heart, soul, mind, and strength. Amen."

✠ Use Meditative Reading as you consider John 11:1-45. Come to the text with the expectation that the Spirit wants to communicate vital truth to your heart. Read the sentences with a quick willingness to review anything that makes an impression upon you. After each paragraph, pause to talk to the Lord about the verse or verses you just read. Express thanks, praise, questions, or confusion to him. Seek to have an interactive experience, pausing for a response when you ask a question. Also, try to sense the significance of the extraordinary claims of the words of Jesus: "I am the resurrection and the life" (John 11:25-26).

✠ As you identify a main point of interest, consider what type of insight it is: Principle (P), Attachment (A), Interior (I), or Detachment (D).

✠ Continue to be sensitive to any emotions you experience during the prayer exercise, and be grateful for consolations as special gifts of grace from God.

✠ Should the text remind you of or reveal to you a need for God's assistance in some area of your life, ask the Lord for his help using a Prayer of Petition.

✠ Express praise, admiration, and love to the Lord in the Prayer of Adoration. Then, sit humbly and gratefully in the Lord's presence in the Prayer of Rest. Quietly enjoy his presence for ten minutes. As your mind wanders, bring it back gently by returning to your insight, or to your Motivating Statement, or to the "Jesus Prayer." Remember, your aim is to achieve a deeper sense of fellowship with Jesus.

✠ Review your prayer exercise, noting those things you did which proved to be beneficial.

Day Two: *"Jesus Anointed"*

<u>Objective</u>: Intimate knowledge of Christ that I might be *with* him, become *like* him, and live *for* him.

<u>Scripture</u>: Mark 14:1-11.

<u>First point</u>: Jesus is dining in the home of Simon the Leper.

<u>Second point</u>: A woman anoints Jesus with expensive perfume. She is rebuked harshly.

<u>Third point</u>: Jesus defends her. Judas betrays Jesus.

Your Response:

✣   Plan to use all three types of Mental Prayer in this prayer exercise. After you have asked God for help using the Preparatory Prayer, read the entire account using Meditative Reading, interacting with the Lord at the end of each verse or two. Move on to Imaginative Contemplation by visualizing the entire story from start to finish. Then, consider it from the standpoint of the Prayer of Consideration, seeking an example of each of the four kinds of insights: Principle (P), Attachment (A), Interior (I), or Detachment (D). On which insight does the Lord want you to dwell deeply? Spend time with that insight. Remember that the Holy Spirit may lead you in a direction different from my suggestions. Stay flexible so that you can follow the Spirit's lead.

✣   If you have been moved to desire a particular quality or virtue that you see in Jesus, use the Prayer of Petition to make a special request to the Lord.

✣   Assuming that you have been led to an insight that has given you intimate knowledge of Christ, adore the Lord in the Prayer of Adoration. Then sit humbly and gratefully in his presence in the Prayer of Rest for ten minutes.

✣   Review your prayer period, noting whether you were sensitive to Heart Prayer and gave thanks for it.

Day Three: "Palm Sunday"

<u>Objective</u>: Intimate knowledge of Christ that I might be *with* him, become *like* him, and live *for* him.

<u>Scripture</u>: Luke 19:28-44.

<u>First point</u>: The Lord sent two disciples for the colt. Jesus instructed them to say, "The Lord needs it."

<u>Second point</u>: Jesus rode the colt.

<u>Third point</u>: Jesus wept over Jerusalem.

Your Response:

❖ Using a Preparatory Prayer, ask for God's help to achieve the objective of this prayer exercise.

❖ Using the Prayer of Imaginative Contemplation, visualize this story. Sense the initial confusion of disciples as they were instructed by Jesus, the excitement they felt when they found the colt where Jesus told them it would be, the submission of the owners when they heard the words, "The Lord needs it."

Be part of the crowd and spread your cloak on the road in front of the colt Jesus is riding. See him look into your eyes as he passes by. Join in the celebration. See yourself shouting joyfully with a loud voice, "Blessed is the king who comes in the name of the Lord! Peace in heaven and glory in the highest!" (Luke 19:38).

❖ Be conscious of any consolations that you may feel. Stay with them as long as they last, and give thanks to the Lord for them.

❖ Seek to find one Attachment Insight (A) that you can meditate upon deeply. Ask yourself, "What in the text moves me to want to attach myself to Christ?"

❖ Offer praise to the Lord through the Prayer of Adoration.

❖ Abide humbly and gratefully in the presence of the Lord in the Prayer of Rest. The sooner you can move away from the images of the story to a sense of oneness with Christ, the better. As your mind wanders, bring your thoughts back by returning to your insight or to the "Jesus Prayer."

❖ Review your prayer exercise to determine the extent to which you fulfilled the objective.

Day Four: *"Jesus Cleanses the Temple"*

Objective: Intimate knowledge of Christ that I might be *with* him, become *like* him, and live *for* him.

Scripture: Mark 11:12-25.

First point: Jesus reacts to the unfruitfulness of the fig tree.

Second point: Jesus drives out those who were buying and selling in the temple area and quotes Scripture: "My house will be called a house of prayer for all nations."

Third point: Jesus draws lessons from the withered fig tree.

Your Response:

Let the Spirit lead you.

Day Five: *"Four Degrees of Humility"*

Objective: Desire to be totally influenced by Jesus Christ.

Background: The "Four Degrees of Humility" is presented as an ideal which Jesus achieved and which Ignatius provided as a goal for those willing to be completely influenced by Christ. To be humble is to have a submissive attitude toward God. It is the opposite of being proud or arrogant. Humility expresses itself in a spirit of deference, just as Jesus "humbled himself and became obedient to death — even death on a cross" (Philippians 2:8). Since we are to live according to the pattern of his life, we also are to seek after humility that we might be as much like him as he enables us to be.

Because of the length of this meditation, it is advisable to divide it into two consecutive prayer periods: consider the first two degrees of humility during this prayer exercise on day five; the second two during the prayer exercise on day six. Some people prefer to do the entire exercise in one sitting and use the *"Repeat"* session, which is the prayer exercise for day six, for a more thorough concentration on the points that need special attention.

First Degree of Humility. The first kind of humility consists of humbling yourself in such a way that you are willing to come under the law of God in all things. Thus, even if you were given all authority, power, and wealth, you would not consent to an intentional violation of one of the Ten Commandments.

Scripture: Exodus 20:3-17.

Your Response:

> ✜ Use Preparatory Prayer to ask for God's help to achieve the objective of the First Degree of Humility. Example: "Dear Lord, how grateful I am for your love for me. Because of your abiding love, I find that I have a growing love for you. Please enable me to demonstrate my love by giving me a deep desire to keep your commandments. I truly want to be fully influenced by you. Amen."

> ✜ Use the Prayer of Consideration as you read the Scripture passage, Exodus 20:3-17, in light of the First Degree of Humility statement expressed above. Instead of looking for the four types of insights (PAID), reflect on the objective of the prayer period and the requirements of the first kind of humility. Consider the implications of being totally influenced by Christ. Placing yourself before the Lord, consider how much he loves you (John 15:9). Acknowledge that nothing in the world is worth even a single violation of one of the Ten Commandments.

Second Degree of Humility. The second kind of humility is higher than the first. You possess it if your attitude of mind is such that in wanting to give priority to seeking and doing the will of your Father, you do not prefer, and feel no inclination to have, a luxurious lifestyle over a simple lifestyle, honor over dishonor, a long life over a short life, control over giving up control.

Scripture: Philippians 3:7-21; 4:10-19.

Your Response:

❖ Pray through Philippians 3:7-21; 4:10-19 and ponder its message in light of this second kind of humility. An attitude of detachment is extremely important as you move from the first degree of humility to the second. Place yourself before the Lord, who graciously gives you strength (Philippians 4:13) and all blessings (Ephesians 1:3), and ask for the grace to possess this second degree of humility.

Third Degree of Humility. The third kind of humility consists of humbling yourself so that you will not want to turn away from God even in what may be considered minor ways. Your whole desire should be to respond ever more faithfully to his great love for you. You would, therefore, not consent for all creation to an intentional violation of what might be considered a minor sin, such as a lack of charity. The Third Degree of Humility presupposes the detachment required in the second degree since a longing for wealth, honor, a long life, and control or power can easily override your intentions to be genuinely charitable.

Scripture: 1 Corinthians 13:1-8a; Matthew 5:21-48

Your Response:

❖ Use the Prayer of Consideration as you explore the implications of 1 Corinthians 13:1-8a in view of the third kind of humility. Place yourself before the Lord. Indicate to him that you would be willing to humble yourself so that even if you were given all authority, power, and wealth, you would not consent to an intentional violation of what might be considered a minor sin; that is, engaging in a lack of charity.

Fourth Degree of Humility. This is the highest kind of humility. It indicates that you so much want to respond to God's love that you earnestly desire to live according to the pattern of Christ. Consequently, whenever the praise and glory of God would be equally served, you would prefer a simple lifestyle with Christ who was poor rather than an extravagant life of worldly riches. You would prefer insults with Christ who was dishonored rather than honors. You would prefer to be considered worthless and a fool for Christ rather than to be esteemed as wise and prudent according to the standards of this world.

Scripture: 2 Corinthians 12:7-10; Philippians 3:7-11.

Your Response:

> ❖ This fourth degree of humility presupposes that sin is not a central concern. In this humility you are dealing with something other than the law and moral obligations. At issue is the complete willingness to be influenced by Christ. The important thing is to ask whether your desire is sufficiently elevated so that your choice is always to be with Christ wherever he is, even when he is found among the poor, among insults and humiliations, and among those who are rejected and despised.
>
> Thomas H. Green pointed out that either you love Christ that much or you do not. You can desire it, but you cannot make it happen.[7] What can you do? You can use the Prayer of Petition to ask God to choose you for that kind of devotion, that degree of humility, so that you might better imitate Christ; that is, be more like him and serve him more wholeheartedly.
>
> ❖ Ponder this fourth degree of humility in light of 2 Corinthians 12:7-10 and Philippians 3:8-11. Seek to be completely influenced by Christ.

Day Six: "Repeat"

A frequent choice for those in this prayer program is to use this *"Repeat"* prayer period to cover in greater detail the *"Four Degrees of Humility"* or to use it for the final two degrees of humility if only the first two degrees were considered in prayer period five.

Day Seven: "Review"

Review all of the prayer exercises of this week, asking the Lord for a unifying message that he may have been communicating to you.

FRIENDS ON THE JOURNEY

Bob — Desire for more consolations

Bob was receiving helpful insights during his prayer time, but felt disappointed that he was not experiencing significant consolations. I reminded him of the consolations to which he had referred with great joy only the week before and suggested that he review his journal regularly so as to not forget the good gifts of consolation that God had already given him.

This led to a discussion of how the experience of consolations varies with each individual. I indicated that emotional responses differ according to a person's temperament, his or her psychological health (a "gift of tears" may be the real thing or repressed feelings of grief that need to be worked through), or even the effect of the culture from which a person comes. One would have a more difficult time receiving consolations in prayer if raised in a family, community, or church with an anti-emotional attitude and perspective.

An additional factor is that some people have fewer consolations because God is leading them to a higher experience of faith. It is best to receive consolations gratefully when they come but to remain undisturbed if they do not. Either way, the key is to be detached. One must learn to receive or not to receive as the Father determines.

Cathy — Don't change course in desolation!

Cathy had a bad week. She interviewed for a new job, but nothing came of it. She felt defeated, was angry with God, and wanted to give up on the prayer program.

I reminded her of the important spiritual principles discussed in the beginning of this chapter: when a person is experiencing discouragement or some other form of desolation, she should avoid changing a decision that was made before the onset of desolation. The reason is that for the committed person, desolation is not God's voice.

It would be a terrible mistake, I told Cathy, to leave the prayer program after six weeks because of the frustration that had suddenly come into her life. She needed to remain with the original decision made six weeks before.

Instead of quitting the prayer program, I urged her to make use of her free time by drawing closer to the Lord and praying just as long as she had been praying or even longer. I also reminded her that the discouragement would lift and that God would bless her and fulfill his plan to give her life, joy, and peace! She agreed to stay with it.

PART III
The Suffering of Christ

Part III brings us to the suffering, crucifixion, and death of Christ. The final days of the earthly life of Jesus provide us with a unique opportunity to understand more fully the courage, compassion, and grace with which Jesus bore the most grievous suffering. If we believe that he endured everything out of love for us and for our sins, we will be drawn to an ever more profound love of him. Our prayer during this week of exercises will be for empathy, sorrow, and adoration. We will be assisted in our meditations by following the guidelines on eating presented in Week 7.

.

WEEK 7
EATING ACCORDING TO
SPIRITUAL PERSPECTIVES

In Week 7, we have the opportunity to deepen our understanding of God's love for us as we consider how Jesus suffered and died for each of us (Romans 5:8; Hebrews 2:9; Ephesians 5:2; 1 John 3:16). To meditate with heightened spiritual perception on this sacred theme, guidelines are provided that encourage us to cut back on our diet. The guidelines called *"Eating According to Spiritual Perspectives"* are beneficial not only during this special week when we consider the passion of Christ, but also beyond this prayer program. They indicate what and how we should eat so that we can gain mastery over our bodies with regard to food.

Controlling one's diet is a formidable objective, not only for those who give their appetites free reign, but also for those who brake their appetites on a regular basis. As Dallas Willard observed, our bodies are powerful and shrewd in getting their own way against our strongest resolves.[1]

Ignatius, keenly aware of how our appetites tend to go to excess, taught that Satan was constantly at work using food to defeat us through temptations. Accordingly, he provided a list of recommendations that take us beyond the exercise of willpower. Ignatius' eight-point plan is a matched and durable set, which provides a long-term strategy for achieving mastery over one's eating habits.

Ignatius' rules for eating need to be seen in the larger context of his *Spiritual Exercises,* which have as their stated purpose "the conquest of self and the regulation of one's life in such a way that no decision is made under the influence of any inordinate attachment."[2] Mastery over food serves as an example of this. It results in an ability to satisfy one's need for food and enjoyment of food without yielding to compulsive or addictive behavior.

LESS FOOD, GREATER LIGHT

For the Present: Greater Light during Week 7 Exercises

If we deny the physical, we will quicken the spiritual, receiving more illumination and a deeper sense of God's presence. This spiritual principle is especially important during Week 7 when we turn to the sacred narratives describing the passion of our Lord. The amount and kind of food we eat and the manner in which we eat it will make a difference in our ability to enter sensitively into the rich Gospel narratives of the events of Holy Week.

It may be helpful to show that many traditions of Christian spirituality acknowledge this principle. In his influential book, *Celebration of Discipline*, Richard Foster pointed out that bringing one's appetites under control has long been recognized as a means by which one can increase effectiveness in prayer, revelations, and concentration.[3]

The Eastern Orthodox writer from Finland, Tito Colliander, warned that according to the ascetics, "one should not ponder divine matters on a full stomach.... For the well-fed even the most superficial secrets of the Trinity lie hidden."[4]

The Swiss Reformer John Calvin insisted that fasting enables us to be better prepared for "prayers and holy meditations." He appealed to common wisdom: "Surely we experience this: with a full stomach our mind is not so lifted up to God that it can be drawn to prayer with a serious and ardent affection and persevere in it."[5]

Though Martin Luther was known for his eating and drinking, he also cautioned that when "the stomach is full, the body does not serve for preaching, for praying, for studying, or for doing anything else that is good. Under such circumstances God's Word cannot remain."[6]

The Lutheran churchman of the 1940s, Dietrich Bonhoeffer insisted, "When the flesh is satisfied it is hard to pray with cheerfulness or to devote oneself to a life of service which calls for much self-renunciation."[7]

For the Future: Harmony and Order in Our Dietary Habits

The guidelines are also provided to bring harmony and order to our eating habits beyond this eight-week program. This is not for the purpose of gaining merit with God. We are saved by grace through faith (Ephesians 2:8-9). Nor are the guidelines an attempt to impose an arbitrary long-term asceticism. Rather, they help us become masters over our bodily appetites, a fundamental aim of the Apostle Paul's teaching: "I will not be mastered by anything" (1 Corinthians 6:12).

Our Lord spoke as though it were within the power of his disciples not only to cut back on their food intake but to do so in such a way that others would not notice. He voiced this expectation in the Sermon on the Mount, saying:

> When you fast, put oil on your head and wash your face, so that it will not be obvious to men that you are fasting, but only to your Father, who is unseen; and your Father, who sees what is done in secret, will reward you (Matthew 6:17-18).

Commenting on this passage, Dietrich Bonhoeffer expressed the following two convictions: "Jesus takes it for granted that His disciples will observe the pious custom of fasting. Strict exercise of self-control is an essential feature of the Christian's life."[8]

Why is self-control as an ongoing discipline so important? Because the opposite of self-control is self-indulgence, and that is nothing less than bowing to the god of our appetite (Philippians 3:19). Cornelius Plantinga wrote:

> Self-indulgence is the enemy of gratitude, and self-discipline usually its friend and generator. That is why gluttony is a deadly sin. The early desert fathers believed that a person's appetites are linked: full stomachs and jaded palates take the edge from our hunger and thirst for righteousness. They spoil the appetite for God.[9]

By experience, we know that culinary pleasures have a seductive power. They can take over and choke the word (Mark 4:19). On the other hand, as Thomas à Kempis pointed out, self-discipline can pay rich dividends: "Bridle thy riotous appetite, and thou shalt be the better able to keep under all the unruly motions of the flesh."[10]

If our goal were to develop a strong body through weight training and aerobics, we would go on a diet that would support that physical purpose. But the goal that is set before us is devotion to God. Ignatius' guidelines support that spiritual purpose.

MASTERY OVER WHAT AND HOW YOU EAT

What then are Ignatius' "Rules with Regard to Eating"?[11] I have taken the liberty of paraphrasing them in the first person singular and italicizing them. Following my restatement of each of Ignatius' rules, I have added commentary that supports and/or illustrates his guidelines.

1. Enjoy bread

I can eat bread with less concern since my appetite is not stirred up as acutely by it, nor is temptation as insistent when eating bread as with other kinds of foods.

In this first rule, the underlying issue is appetite stimulation. This is an inward desire that responds to our sense of hunger but which can also be aroused by psychological, social, or spiritual factors. Since natural grain bread does not activate the craving for more food in the same way as other more palatable foods, Ignatius concluded that it does not generally lead to over-indulgence.

2. Choose beverages that are helpful

Beverages require greater care than bread. I need to consider carefully what would be helpful, and therefore to be included in my diet; and what would be harmful, and therefore to be avoided.

Since we desire mastery over ourselves, we evaluate beverages in terms of whether they lead to self-control or to over-indulgence. There will be differences between individuals, and each must follow his or her judgment based upon experience and self-knowledge.

It makes sense to develop an appreciation for water and to drink six to eight or more glasses of water a day. This will help us cut back on beverages that may be addictive to us personally (coffee, cola, alcohol).

3. Cultivate a preference for staples

I should be conscious that the appetite tends more readily to be excessive and temptation to be insistent when considering the wide variety of food available to me. To avoid disorder in eating these foods, abstinence can be practiced in two ways:

(a) *By developing a greater dependence on the staples within the diet.*

(b) *By eating sparingly of rich and delicate food.*

Because of the cravings of the appetite and the temptations to overeat, we should cultivate a preference for staples such as whole grains, legumes, vegetables, and fruit. This is advice offered not only by Ignatius in the sixteenth century but by many reputable physicians in America. Neal Barnard, M. D., President of the Physicians Committee for Responsible Medicine, recommends that our diet be based on the new four food groups: whole grain flour products such as pasta, bread, and tortillas; legumes such as beans, peas, and lentils; a wide assortment of vegetables such as potatoes, sweet potatoes, and yams; and fruit.[12] The result is reduction in fat intake and an increase in fiber, complex carbohydrates, and other important nutrients.

"Delicacies" are to be eaten sparingly according to Ignatius. Again, there is agreement among health professionals who tell us that pies, cakes, and pastries are filled with whole milk products, butter, margarine, vegetable shortening, and products made with tropical oils and partially hydrogenated oils. The universal advice of physicians is that we decrease foods in our diet made with these products.

Because of the example of Jesus, I side with those who do not exclude meat, fish, and dairy products. After all, Jesus fed fish to his disciples on several occasions and featured a fatted calf as the main course for the feast celebrating the return of the "prodigal son" (Luke 15:23).

Diets of whole grains, green vegetables, fruit, pasta, olive oil, and the occasional use of meat and low-to-moderate amounts of fish and chicken continue to be the Mediterranean diet. Findings from the Lyon Diet Heart

145

Study were published in 1994 showing that test subjects with heart disease reduced the risk of a second heart attack by 50 to 70 percent if they followed the diet. A second wave of data from the study was released in 1999 bolstering earlier findings.[13] Jesus, himself, presumably ate a typical Mediterranean diet in his day. And that diet was probably similar to the diet served in that part of the world today.

4. Reduce food intake

*Provided care is taken not to fall sick, the more I reduce my intake from a sufficient diet, the more speedily I will arrive at the mean I should observe in the matter of food and drink.** Two reasons for this are:*

> *First, by reducing my diet, I will often experience more consolations and divine movements within my spirit and these may confirm me in the appropriate amount of food I should eat.*
>
> *Second, if I perceive that a diet does not provide sufficient strength and health for the Spiritual Exercises, I can increase my intake so that my strength is increased.*

Ignatius is talking about fasting, which means that a person deprives himself to some degree of normal foods for a certain period of time. A variety of motives could be cited for fasting. A major spiritual incentive is that fasting provides an opportunity to experience spiritual nourishment in place of physical nourishment, as Jesus indicated to his disciples at the Samaritan well.

> Meanwhile his disciples urged him, "Rabbi, eat something."
>
> But he said to them, "I have food to eat that you know nothing about."
>
> Then his disciples said to each other, "Could someone have brought him food?"
>
> "My food," said Jesus, "is to do the will of him who sent me and to finish his work" (John 4:31-34).

** Senior citizens and others who have dietary requirements should consult their physicians before making dietary changes.

Jesus' physical needs were being met by spiritual sources. This has profound significance for those who desire intimacy with Christ. If we combine the discipline of fasting with meditation on his Word, God can nourish our souls and sustain us physically despite a reduction in the food we eat. We obviously cannot go for long without physical nourishment. Our bodies require physical food and are adept at letting us know when more nourishment is necessary.

Spiritual motivation to abstain from food, which has wide advocacy among Christian leaders of every age, can be very compelling. The English evangelist of the Great Awakening, John Wesley, viewed fasting as a help to private prayer. He also saw it as "a means in the hand of God of confirming and increasing ... seriousness of spirit, earnestness, sensibility and tenderness of conscience, deadness to the world, and consequently the love of God, and every holy and heavenly affection."[14]

The English spiritual writer William Law explained the benefits of reducing our intake from a sufficient diet:

> If religion requires us sometimes to fast and deny our natural appetites, it is to lessen that struggle and war that is in our nature; it is to render our bodies fitter instruments of purity, and more obedient to the good motions of divine grace; it is to dry up the springs of our passions that war against the soul, to cool the flame of our blood, and render the mind more capable of divine meditations. So that although these abstinences [sic] give some pain to the body, yet they so lessen the power of bodily appetites and passions, and increase our taste of spiritual joys, that even these severities [sic] of religion, when practiced with discretion, add much to the comfortable enjoyment of our lives.[15]

Fasting is being practiced in contemporary religious movements around the world. Dr. Bill Bright, President and Founder of Campus Crusade for Christ, challenged two million Christians in North America to fast for 40 days and to pray for worldwide revival for the fulfillment of the Great Commission.[16] The plan is admirable, but those who engage in it must be careful not to attract attention to themselves. The Lord instructed us to fast in secret so that we would practice this discipline in obedience to him and not to impress others.

On a more moderate scale, we can skip a meal or two or three each week or reduce daily calories for the spiritual purposes mentioned above.

Our spirits and bodies respond favorably to this type of disciplined fasting, often with feelings of enthusiasm and well being. If that is not the case, if fasting becomes a problem for us with headaches or dizziness, we should not do it. We should aim instead at eating moderately since overeating leaves us spiritually sluggish and drowsy and leads to obesity and a host of other health problems.

5. Imagine Jesus at the table

While I am eating, I imagine I see Jesus at the table. I consider how he eats and drinks, how he looks and speaks, and then strive to imitate him. In this way my mind is occupied principally with our Lord and less with food. This leads to greater harmony and orderliness in the way I conduct myself during meals.

In this mealtime engagement of imaginative contemplation, we must be careful to follow the biblical representation of Jesus as a loving, compassionate person who enjoyed the company of common people, and not as one who looked across the table in a stern or disapproving manner. One of the descriptions he gave of himself was that of a friendly dinner companion: "The Son of Man came eating and drinking" (Luke 7:33-34).

I practice this fifth guideline not only as suggested, but also by finding Christ in the expressions and words of those at the table with me. He, after all, indwells all who believe in him; and the image of the Creator is on all, no matter how distorted that image has become through disobedience. By seeing Jesus in others, I am more likely to treat them as I would treat him.

6. Turn attention away from food to other matters

While eating, I can occupy myself with various considerations such as an article or book, a project on which I am working, a conversation with a friend, or music in the background. When I shift my attention to these things, I focus less on the gratification I experience from food.

Since preoccupation with the food on our plates can lead to loss of control, it is wise to direct our attention elsewhere. If we are eating out, we can notice the ambiance of the restaurant, be more aware of those around us, engage in polite dinner conversation, slow down by sipping a beverage, listen to background music, or pause after each bite to put down our knife and fork. In these ways we extend the length of time at the table, giving our digestive processes time to communicate the feeling of fullness, the God-given signal that tells us we have eaten enough.

7. Strive for self-control

Most important of all, my goal must be to be master of myself, both in the manner in which I eat and in the amount I eat. I do that by being on guard against concentrating exclusively upon what I am eating and against being carried away by my appetite so that I eat hurriedly.

This is the most important of the eight points because it corresponds to the purpose of the Spiritual Exercises: the conquest of self. To be in control of our behavior, to act or not to act according to right intentions, to be able to restrain cravings and other compulsive behaviors are evidences of spiritual growth.

Therefore, while we are eating, it is not enough for us to turn our attention on other matters as point six advises. We must pray earnestly for the grace of self-control and for a greater desire to be masters of ourselves. If, instead, we are titillated and overcome by the look, smell, and taste of food, we will most likely lose control of both the amount and the manner in which we eat.

Many of us are aware of those times when we concentrated excessively on the food before us. Time and again we satisfied our out-of-control appetite and all too often the consequence of stuffing ourselves was guilt, stomach pains in the night, and renewed determination to bring our appetite under control.

8. *Determine the amount for the next meal*

Finally, comes the all-important rule for limiting the amount of food to be eaten during the next meal. After dinner or at any time when I do not desire food, I arrange for the next dinner or supper, so every day fix the amount that is proper for me to eat. It is absolutely crucial not to exceed this amount, regardless of my appetite or the temptation.

The first four guidelines deal with the kind and amount of food to be eaten. They are to be kept in mind as we turn to this final guideline and decide on what and how much we will eat at our next meal. The decision needs to be made at a time when we do not desire food.

Through the years I have tried a variety of diets that have helped me move toward moderation in eating. Finding a diet that works for you will enable you to satisfy your hunger and provide you with energy and a sense of well-being until the next meal.

This can help you with the final guideline. It tells us that "it is absolutely crucial" to resist any temptation to increase the amount of food that we have decided for the next meal. Only by sticking to the designated amount, no matter what our appetite or the temptation, will we achieve mastery over our eating habits.

SEVEN PRAYER EXERCISES

Along with dietary changes, it will be helpful during this week to ask with special intensity for God's help to prepare us for the meditations that take us step by step to the hallowed cross of Christ. The opportunity for significant insight and deeply felt devotion is very great as we observe the Son of God during the following Prayer Exercises: *"Last Supper," "Gethsemane," "Arrest and Jewish Trials," "Peter's Denial," "Roman Trials," "Crucifixion and Seven Last Words,"* and *"Death and Burial."*

It would be especially beneficial to meditate on these Week 7 exercises during the week that begins with Palm Sunday and continues to Easter. You can do that by repeating the Week 7 material during Holy Week in the coming year.

By this time in the prayer program, I assume that you will be able to proceed on your own. Except for the first exercise, I give only a few suggestions on your prayer responses to the remaining six exercises. If you need additional help, refer to the process comments of earlier prayer exercises that you found to be helpful.

Day One: "Last Supper"

Objective: Intimate knowledge of Christ that I might be *with* him, become *like* him, and live *for* him.

Scripture: Matthew 26:17-35; John 13:1-17.

First point: Jesus eats with his disciples and speaks of the betrayal (Matthew 26:17-25).

Second point: He washes the feet of the disciples (John 13:1-17).

Third point: Jesus says, "Take eat, this is my body…. Drink from it, all of you. This is my blood of the covenant, which is poured out for many for the forgiveness of sins" (Matthew 26:26-28).

Your Response:

- Use a Preparatory Prayer to ask for the Lord's help to achieve the objective of this prayer exercise.

- First Point: Use Meditative Reading as you read and pray through Matthew 26:17-25. Meditate on the words, phrases, or thoughts which make an impression on you, trouble you, or inspire you. Talk to the Lord about these thoughts and whatever else sparks your interest. Be conscious of any consolations that you may feel during the prayer exercise.

- Second point: Use Imaginative Contemplation on John 13:1-17. See Jesus pick up the towel, pour water into a basin, and begin to wash the disciples' feet. Observe Peter as he objects and then switches to deferential compliance. After Jesus washes the feet of the disciples, let him wash your feet as well. See him look up into your face with an expression of love in his eyes.

- Third point: Go back to Meditative Reading for Matthew 26:26-29. Concentrate on the words of institution of the Lord's Supper: "Take eat, this is my body…. Drink from it, all of you. This is my blood of the covenant, which is poured out for many for the forgiveness of sins."

- As you consider the main insight that has come to you from each of the three points, take a moment to identify it as one of the four types of insights: Principle (P), Attachment (A),

Interior (I), or Detachment (D). If you have three different insights, one for each of the three points, ask the Holy Spirit to guide you to the one you should focus on most especially.

✣ Assuming that you have been led to an insight that has enabled you to be strengthened by the example of Jesus, use the Prayer of Petition to ask the Lord to make you more *like* him in the particular quality that has inspired you.

✣ Using the Prayer of Adoration, join the grand paean of praise going on in heaven even now and express your love and adoration to the Lord.

✣ Abide with him for several minutes in the Prayer of Rest.

✣ Review your prayer period by considering how well you achieved the objective of the prayer exercise. Did you gain intimate knowledge of Christ? Did you sense that you were *with* Christ during the exercise and that you were with him in a more intentional way during the Prayer of Rest? Did you conclude your session by giving yourself in service *for* the Lord? If not, take a moment to do that now.

Day Two: "Gethsemane"

Objective: Intimate knowledge of Christ that I might be *with* him, become *like* him, and live *for* him.

Scripture: Matthew 26:31-46; Luke 22:39-46.

First point: Jesus goes to Gethsemane with his disciples (Matthew 26:36-38).

Second point: He is in great anguish (Luke 22:39-46).

Third point: Jesus prays three times to the Father, "My Father, if it is possible, may this cup be taken from me. Yet not as I will, but as you will" (Matthew 26:39-46).

Your Response:

In the account of Jesus' prayer in Gethsemane, Jesus shows us how to act when we are confronted with the prospect of rejection and suffering. Begin this session with a Preparatory Prayer. Ask for understanding and empathy for what Jesus was going through. If you do not have a strong desire to enter into an understanding of his suffering, ask the Lord to give you that desire. God gives us desire when we ask for it earnestly. Then, notice the character qualities of Jesus (Attachment Insights), identify principles that guide conduct (Principle Insights), seek a deeper understanding of who you are (Interior Insights), embrace the call for self-denial (Detachment Insights). Try this prayer exercise without any further coaching from me, but remain sensitive to the direction of the Holy Spirit all the way through to the evaluation. If you need help, review the "Your Response" recommendations for the previous prayer exercise.

Day Three: "Arrest and Jewish Trials"

Objective: Intimate knowledge of Christ that I might be *with* him, become *like* him, and live *for* him.

Center: Use the following hymns or those of your choosing: *"The Old Rugged Cross," "There is a Fountain Filled with Blood."*

Scripture: See Bible passages indicated for each of the three points below.

First point: Jesus is arrested (Matthew 26:47-56).

Second point: Annas questions Jesus (John 18:12-14, 19-24).

Third point: Caiaphas, the high priest, questions Jesus. Jesus is falsely condemned of blasphemy and sentenced to death (Matthew 26:57-67).

Your Response:

Try this prayer exercise on your own. Seek the direction of the Holy Spirit all the way through the review. Using the Prayer of Petition, ask for sorrow, gratitude, and love because the Lord is going to his suffering for your sins. Also ask him to draw you to a more profound love of him by helping you understand that he endured abuse and mistreatment out of love for you.

153

Day Four: "Peter's Denial"

<u>Objective</u>: Intimate knowledge of Christ that I might be *with* him, become *like* him, and live *for* him.

<u>Center</u>: Use the following hymns or those of your choosing *"When I Survey the Wondrous Cross," "Jesus Paid It All."*

<u>Scripture</u>: See Bible passages indicated for each of the three points below.

<u>First point</u>: The first round of denials (Mark 14:66-68).

<u>Second point</u>: The second and third denials (Matthew 26:71-74; John 18:25-27).

<u>Third point</u>: Jesus looks at Peter, and Peter goes out and weeps bitterly (Luke 22:61-62).

Your Response:

You decide. Look to the Spirit. Using the Prayer of Petition, ask for sorrow and shame because the Lord is going to his suffering for your sins.

Day Five: "Roman Trials"

<u>Objective</u>: Intimate knowledge of Christ that I might be *with* him, become *like* him, and live *for* him.

<u>Center</u>: Use the following hymns or others of your choosing: *"Jesus Thy Blood and Righteousness," "And Can It Be that I Should Gain."*

<u>Scripture</u>: See Bible passages indicated for each of the three points below.

<u>First point</u>: Jesus explains his kingdom to Pilate, then keeps silent (John 18:28-38). Use Meditative Reading. Meditate on one major insight.

<u>Second point</u>: Herod treats Jesus with contempt (Luke 23:1-12). Use Prayer of Consideration. Find examples of at least two of the four types of insights.

Third point: Jesus is scourged, mockingly arrayed like a king, sentenced and delivered to the soldiers for execution (Matthew 27:1-2, 11-31). Use Imaginative Contemplation.

Your Response:

Suggestions are included with each of the three points above. Improvise as you see fit. Using the Prayer of Petition, follow the recommendation of Ignatius by asking "for sorrow with Christ in sorrow, anguish with Christ in anguish, tears and deep grief because of the great affliction Christ endures for me."[17]

Day Six: "Crucifixion and Seven Last Words"

Objective: Intimate knowledge of Christ that I might be *with* him, become *like* him, and live *for* him.

Center: Use the following hymns or others you choose: *"Alas and Did My Savior Bleed," "O Sacred Head Now Wounded."*

Scripture: See Bible passages indicated for each of the Seven Words.

Your Response:

Use Meditative Reading and/or Imaginative Contemplation as you consider the seven last words of Christ. Throughout this meditation, recognize that the Lord suffered and died for you personally. Place yourself at the scene of the crucifixion through the Prayer of Imaginative Contemplation. Seek to empathize with the suffering of Jesus, to feel sorrow and adoration. While meditating on one of the seven words, ask Jesus whether he would have given himself in death for your sins if you were the only person in the world. Hear him say "Yes" to you as you commune with him in prayer.

The Seven Last Words are found in the Bible passages cited. Turn to these passages to consider the context in which the words were uttered.

The First Word. Jesus prays for those who crucified him (Luke 23:33-34).

The Second Word. Jesus pardons the thief (Luke 23:38-43).

The Third Word. Jesus provides for Mary (John 19:25-27).

The Fourth Word. Jesus expresses thirst (John 19:28-29).

The Fifth Word. Jesus experiences desolation (Mark 15:33-35).

The Sixth Word. Jesus completes his task (John 19:30).

The Seventh Word. Jesus commits himself to the Father (Luke 23:46).

Day Seven: "Death and Burial"

Objective: Intimate knowledge of Christ that I might be *with* him, become *like* him, and live *for* him.

Scripture: See Bible passages indicated for each of the three points below.

First point: The Veil of the temple is torn in two from top to bottom. Jesus breathes his last (Luke 23:44-49).

Second point: The soldiers pierce his side (John 19:31-37).

Third point: Jesus is taken down from the cross, prepared for burial, and placed in a tomb (John 19:38-42; Luke 23:50-54).

Your Response:

Be led by the Spirit as you meditate on these sacred events and as you draw on your powers to grieve and feel sorry that he suffered all this for your sins.

FRIENDS ON THE JOURNEY

Bob — Fasting one day a week

After reading my comments on "Eating According to Spiritual Perspectives," Bob decided that he wanted to fast for a period of at least 24 hours one day a week. He felt that would draw him closer to God, enable him to grow in self-control, and increase his awareness and concern for those who go to bed hungry every day. He wanted to talk to me about how he could keep from losing motivation.

Fasting for a full day is more comfortable, I suggested, when it is in harmony with the physical processes of one's body. Many people find that it is easier on their digestive and eliminative systems to begin by excluding the evening meal. That means missing supper on the first day and going without food until supper on the next day. The other most common alternative is to skip breakfast, lunch, and supper on the same day and not eat until the following morning. I suggested that Bob experiment to see which worked better for him.

Next, I recommended that Bob keep in mind some of the major biblical reasons for fasting. The Bible indicates that fasting is a way of receiving nourishment directly from God (John 4:34), of developing self-mastery so that we can serve God in spiritual freedom (1 Corinthians 9:27), and of expressing our longing for the return of Jesus (Matthew 9:14-17). It is also appropriate to fast for guidance (Acts 13:1-4), spiritual recovery (1 Samuel 7:6), and grace to handle difficulties (Luke 4:1-2).

As I spoke with Bob, I felt the need to warn him against telling others about his plan. Jesus indicated that his followers should fast (Matthew 6:16-18; 9:14-15) and that their fasting would be rewarded by the Father (Matthew 6:18), but he clearly instructed them to fast in secret (Matthew 6:16-18) so as not to advertise their "acts of righteousness" (Matthew 6:1).

I also felt it would be helpful to point out that Ignatius did not provide his instruction on eating and fasting until Part III of the exercises. He reserved this topic, in other words, for those who had demonstrated a serious desire to work through the exercises and who, in fact, had done so to a large extent. That would indicate, I suggested to Bob, that he not offer casual advice to friends who might not be ready for or receptive to the ideas on eating and fasting presented in this chapter. Instead, he could simply enjoy eating with friends, as Jesus did, without giving advice unless asked by a thoughtful inquirer.

Cathy — Devotions each and every day?

Cathy said that she felt God was actively wooing her. "My motivation climbed this week," she said. "I feel like the Lord is drawing me more and more. But I had difficulty doing all seven prayer exercises."

That led her to ask: "Is it really necessary to have seven sessions? Why not four or five?" She reminded me that in the physical realm it is not necessary to exercise every day but only three or four times a week. "Wouldn't it also be better," she asked, "to rest two or three days each week in the spiritual realm?"

The analogy doesn't hold up, I explained, because to be with Christ whom we love should not result in tension or stress from which we would need relief. We can vary our approach to God, but we must not neglect the love relationship. Personal time with the Lord, if engaged in properly, becomes a daily delight. Admittedly, there are times when our flesh resists devotions. That is why our time of prayer must also become a daily habit. I assured Cathy that as she continued in Devotional Prayer and, especially, as she learned to rest in the Lord, her time of communion with Christ would become the highlight of her day.

PART IV

The Resurrection of Christ

We began in Part I by seeking an increase in self-understanding. Then, in Part II, we grew in intimate knowledge of Christ and deepened our love for Jesus and our desire to serve him. That commitment was strengthened in Part III as we meditated on his passion and considered anew how he suffered and died for us individually out of his great love for us. Now, in Part IV, we have the opportunity to ponder the great and triumphant truth that Jesus conquered death, and that because he lives, we also live with him now and eternally.

Part IV invites us to be glad and rejoice intensely in the glory of Christ our resurrected Lord who promises never to leave us and who empowers us to obey him in all that he has taught us. Instruction is also provided showing how we can use Devotional Prayer to meditate on every portion of the Bible.

WEEK 8

CHARTING YOUR PRAYER FUTURE

In Week 8, we will be meditating on the Scriptures that deal with the glorious resurrection of Jesus Christ. These passages of the Bible help us understand the majesty of our victorious Lord and enable us to relate to our family, friends, and neighbors with radiant joy as we recognize that "He is risen indeed!" But first, in this final week, I will anticipate questions you may have regarding your devotions in the months and years to come. I will describe the way in which the entire Bible is available for your continued use in Devotional Prayer. I also will discuss some of the ways in which you can test your progress in spiritual development.

A Process that Leads to Discipleship

It will be helpful to remember the purpose of this prayer program. Throughout these eight weeks, my desire has been to lead you through a process that would increase your intimacy with Christ while at the same time decrease your reliance on me as your spiritual mentor. I have encouraged flexibility throughout, not wanting to squeeze everyone into the same mold. Mental effort and a methodical approach were necessary, but only as an initial learning process. As you gained proficiency with prayer principles and skills, you became more sensitive to the guidance of the Holy Spirit. My hope is that, having begun well through this prayer course, you will continue to grow in your reliance on the Spirit as your Spiritual Director.

I have encouraged you to seek the counsel and assistance of human teachers and guides since the Lord, himself, provides these persons for your benefit. But I have counseled you to keep firmly in mind that God alone is the ultimate Teacher of prayer.

The foundation of a life of devoted service rests upon intimacy *with* Christ. The prayer program has taught us to seek insights that focus on the goodness and grace of Jesus rather than on our deficiencies (as explained in the Introduction and Week 3). It has guided us to spend time in restful communion *with* Christ (as explained in Week 4). It has encouraged us to persist in prayer when dryness and discouragement burden us (as discussed in Week 5). It has taught us to discern the will of God with patient, prayerful neutrality (as explained in Week 6). And it has urged us to receive more light by achieving mastery over our eating habits (as described in Week 7).

The development of intimacy with Christ has also required that we become aware of the deceptions of greed, power, and the praise of others. Also stressed was the importance of freedom from everything that would keep us from knowing and doing the will of God. Ignatius' thematic meditations — "Most Appealing" (p. 49), "Two Banners" (p. 73), "Three Types of Persons" (p. 93), and "Four Degrees of Humility" (p. 132) — instructed and challenged us. These meditations, when thoroughly pondered and assimilated into our value systems, release us from the attractions and attitudes that erode wholehearted commitment to Jesus.

Toward the end of the eight-week training program, I normally ask participants to evaluate their prayer experience. The responses are usually very positive. For example, when asked to comment on one or two of the most beneficial things they have learned, many who have engaged in the prayer experience make statements like the following. A Presbyterian pastor wrote:

> The spiritual exercises have changed my devotional life forever. I am now spending more time with the Lord than ever before and loving every minute of it. The new ways of praying and reading the Bible have opened a door for me into a deeper relationship with the Lord. Specifically the exercises have led me to linger longer in the Lord's presence, listening, praying, meditating, and learning from Him in ways I've never done before.

An enthusiastic Christian woman, new to the faith, wrote:

> The whole experience has been the most "beneficial" (the word is too small) thing I have ever done in my life. You have helped me find a whole new world, a whole new way of life, a whole new state of being.

A Baptist Pastor wrote:

> I grew exponentially from this learning experience.... This book provides simple exercises for Christians not available anywhere else. But it does so much more. It

explains **why** we should practice them, **what** benefits we will have, and **how** to go from novice to natural. This is the only book I have ever seen that helps a Pastor disciple his/her congregation in the art of loving and imitating Jesus. There is nothing else like it.

Each of these individuals appreciated the training in prayer provided in this eight-week program, but each also wondered how to continue on his or her own. Some planned to go through the prayer program a second time. Others wondered whether I had a list of Bible passages that they could use for meditations. Still others wondered whether devotional prayer could be used with other books of the Bible like the prophetic books or the poetry of the Book of Psalms or the didactic passages of the New Testament letters.

PRAYING THROUGH THE BIBLE

The Bible consists of 66 books, each worthy of prayerful consideration as Paul affirms: "All Scripture is God-breathed and is useful for teaching, rebuking, correcting and training in righteousness, so that the man of God may be thoroughly equipped for every good work" (2 Timothy 3:16-17).

Since the early 1970s, a keen interest has developed in narratives, or stories, in relation to Christian theology. Allister E. McGrath, teacher of theology at Oxford University, pointed out that this trend is sometimes referred to as *narrative theology*. McGrath has taken notice of the way in which the Bible tells stories about God and his dealings with us just as much as it makes doctrinal or theological statements about him.[1]

For instance, the Old Testament tells and retells the story of how God led his people out of Egypt into the Promised Land. It also relates stories of battles, love affairs, betrayals, the building of temples, and calamitous sieges, all of which convey the pleasure or displeasure of God. In a similar way, the New Testament tells the story of God's redeeming action in history, this time centering on the life, death, and resurrection of Jesus Christ, then continues with the story of the spread of his teachings in the Mediterranean world.

The abundance of stories in the Bible makes it easy for us to move from the Gospels, with its stories concerning Jesus, into the Book of Acts with its stories of how God developed and grew the church, or to any of the historical books in the Old Testament. In them we will find lucid and impressive accounts of God's dealings with his people. For purposes of prayer, we can approach these passages in much the same way as we approached the Gospel stories exercises in this prayer program.

In addition to narrative accounts, the Old Testament contains poetic literature. From first to last, the Psalms consist of poetry filled with expressions of prayer and praise, speaking *to* God in prayer and speaking *of* God in praise. A rich experience awaits you as you read the Psalms and realize that they are filled with Principle (P), Interior (I), and Detachment (D) Insights but most especially with Attachment Insights (A). For example, if you turn to Psalm 32:1-11 and use the Prayer of Consideration, you will find at least three Attachment Insights (A) and two Principle Insights (P).

The skills you learned in this prayer course will serve you well as you meditate on the Psalms. You have learned to move from Mental Prayer to Heart Prayer or to the Prayer of Petition or the Prayer of Adoration and ultimately to relax in the immediate presence of God as you engage in the Prayer of Rest.

You can approach other wisdom literature, such as Job, Proverbs, and Ecclesiastes, along with the prophetic literature of the Major and Minor Prophets, a few paragraphs at a time for individual prayer periods. I often use a Study Bible while having devotions in books that are less familiar to me. Gaining an understanding of the text or the historical context can be helpful as long as you make Attachment Insights (A) a priority and keep in mind that textual study is supposed to complement and not compete with Devotional Prayer.

The letters in the New Testament explain how the events of the life, death, and resurrection of Jesus are relevant to humankind. They deal with a number of theological topics which were of great concern to first century believers and which continue to be of interest to us today, such as the relationship between Jew and Gentile in God's plan of redemption. They offer ethical guidance and advice on a number of contemporary problems such as the need to root out arrogant pride, greedy immersion in affluence, race prejudice, and hidden forms of sin.

Any one of these New Testament letters is a rich source of wisdom, instruction, and admonition. I recommend the use of Meditative Reading and/or the Prayer of Consideration for the epistles. These two types of

Mental Prayer will lead to the four types of insights (PAID). The insights will, in turn, often stir your emotions in Heart Prayer, move you to the Prayer of Petition and the Prayer of Adoration, and allow you to conclude with a time of quiet communion with the Lord in the Prayer of Rest.

The nature of the Scripture passage will suggest the type of Mental Prayer to be used. As you have experienced, Imaginative Contemplation is most suitable for stories. Meditative Reading can be used with stories or instruction, and is also useful in reading through the poetic literature of the Old Testament like the Psalms or through the prophetic literature like Isaiah. The ease with which Meditative Reading can be used with the various forms of literature found in the Bible has made it the form of Mental Prayer used most commonly through the centuries. The Prayer of Consideration can also be used with any literary format and is especially useful with didactic passages as found in the New Testament letters.

My continuing counsel is that you give highest priority to finding and dwelling on Attachment Insights (A) regardless of the form of Mental Prayer you are using. This will help you avoid the trap of self-focus.

We need to keep coming back to the recommendation made by every reformer including Luther, Calvin, and Wesley, that we meditate on Jesus' earthly life as recorded in the Gospels. A wise and ancient source, St. Teresa of Avila (1515-1582), who is acknowledged as one of the preeminent authorities of the Western Church in the theology of the spiritual life, insisted that we meditate on the humanity of Jesus, that we continue to think about "the favor God granted us in giving us His only Son."[2] Meditating on any part of God's inspired word can be beneficial, but meditating on the Gospels, especially, promotes intimacy with Christ.

This advice — to stay close to the Gospels — needs to be kept in mind when we shift to the Old Testament stories, or to the Psalms or prophets or the New Testament epistles. We must not stay away too long from the stories of the incarnate God, the Word who became flesh and who in an unparalleled manner revealed and continues to reveal the Father to us.

HOW TO TEST SPIRITUAL EXPERIENCES

As you continue your practice of prayer, you will be tempted to think that you are making good progress if you are experiencing an abundance of joy and that you are making poor progress if you are experiencing apathy. But how you feel, whether happy in consolation or restless in desolation, is not the biblical standard for testing spiritual progress.

What is the appropriate test? How can you know if you are making progress spiritually? How can you test the validity of visions that you may see, words of knowledge that may come to you, shaking or trembling that may overtake you, or other emotional and physical experiences? The evidence that Jesus insisted on was not positive or negative emotions, but spiritual fruit. The experiences you have in prayer and in the spiritual realm in general must be tested by the fruit you manifest in everyday life, as a number of Bible passages indicate:

- "I am the vine; you are the branches. If a man remains in me and I in him, he will bear much fruit; apart from me you can do nothing" (John 15:5).
- "Watch out for false prophets. They come to you in sheep's clothing, but inwardly they are ferocious wolves. By their fruit you will recognize them" (Matthew 7:15-16a).
- "Every good tree bears good fruit, but a bad tree bears bad fruit" (Matthew 7:17).
- "But the fruit of the Spirit is love, joy, peace, patience, kindness, goodness, faithfulness, gentleness, and self-control" (Galatians 5:22-23a).

A basic assumption of this prayer program has been that authentic spiritual progress requires that we be *with* Christ, become *like* Christ, and live *for* Christ. We can check our spiritual progress by going to these three phrases and answering the following three questions.

With Christ – "Do I love God more?"

We began this prayer course by reminding ourselves of the absolute priority of the first commandment: "'Love the Lord your God with all your heart and with all your soul and with all your mind.' This is the first and greatest commandment" (Matthew 22:37-38a). I reasoned that we could best fulfill this commandment not by trying harder, but by fixing our eyes on Jesus.

During these past seven weeks, we have learned to contemplate the impressiveness of Jesus, gaze upon his beauty, meditate on his word, rest in his grace, and offer ourselves for his service. We have imagined him washing our feet and looking into our eyes with deep love and affection as we followed the response suggestions in the meditation on the Lord's Supper at the beginning of Week 7. We have learned to spend time speaking to him of our concerns, listening for his answers to our questions, dwelling in his immediate presence at a more intimate level. All of this makes it possible for us to respond with enthusiasm to the question: "Do I love God more?" "Yes!" we can say, with joyful conviction.

This love manifests itself in a variety of ways. For many of us, love for God expresses itself in ardent songs of praise. We find ourselves singing hymns of worship and praise with a new depth of devotion. We read God's Word with greater deference and delight. We are more certain that Jesus is *with* us to guide and strengthen us. We are more aware of his peace within even when we experience sadness or darkness of soul that comes to us from desolation. We give our money more readily and generously to God's work and to God's people. These are indications that we love God, but the most convincing evidence of our love for God is to be able to answer affirmatively the second question — Am I easier to live with?

Like Christ – "Am I easier to live with?"

If we have been spending time *with* Christ, we will be easier to live with because God will conform us more and more into the likeness of his Son (Romans 8:29). To be *like* Christ is to be a person of love for "God is love" (1 John 4:16). And this love is defined in terms of sacrifice. "This is how we know what love is: Jesus Christ laid down his life for us. And we ought to lay down our lives for our brothers" (1 John 3:16). First John goes on to say that "anyone who does not love his brother, whom he has seen, cannot love God, whom he has not seen. And he [God] has given us this command: Whoever loves God must also love his brother" (1 John 4:20-21). These verses bring love for God and love for others together in an insoluble combination.

167

It's easy to fake love when we are interacting socially with others, but not so easy when with the family. To be a loving person in our home means that we are becoming more patient, kind, and courteous; not always "me first"; not erupting in anger; more tolerant; more willing to put up with anything (1 Corinthians 13:4-7). These qualities translate into being easier to live with. If this is not our experience, then our spiritual intake or practice is somehow defective.

If we are becoming more *like* Christ, we will find ourselves willing to give up our will and preferences not only within our own family but also for the sake of others. This is not something that we struggle to do. Rather, we find that the Spirit is transforming us (2 Corinthians 3:18) into the kind of persons who find it increasingly easy to put other persons ahead of ourselves.

Ignatius saw a direct relationship between a person's progress in the spiritual life and a person's surrender of his or her desires and interests. He wrote, "In all that concerns the spiritual life his progress will be in proportion to his surrender of self-love and of his own will and interests."[3]

An inward transformation must take place before we can surrender self-love and our own will and interests. This inward change is possible only as we enter into a living union with Jesus and become filled with God's love. We can facilitate this inward change by engaging in Devotional Prayer and earnestly asking the Lord for this grace. As he enables us to dwell in his love, the powerful love he substitutes for our self-love can be offered to others with humble recognition that it comes from above.

For Christ – "Am I faithfully fulfilling God's call on my life?"

To live our lives *for Christ* means that we give our best in our vocations as Christian men and women. Where we spend the majority of our time is the place to check how faithfully we are fulfilling this choice; and it is a matter of choice, of will, of our determined purpose. We must ask ourselves whether we are conscientiously fulfilling our responsibilities to our families, employers, churches, and communities; whether we are serving as men and women of integrity and compassion as we live not for men but for the Lord (Colossians 3:23). If we can answer these questions affirmatively, we can know with a fairly high degree of assurance that we are being led by the Holy Spirit.

To live responsibly *for* Christ, we must also take into account two special instructions the Lord gave to his disciples. The first has to do with helping those in need. Jesus said:

> I was hungry and you gave me something to eat, I was thirsty and you gave me something to drink, I was a stranger and you invited me in, I needed clothes and you clothed me, I was sick and you looked after me, I was in prison   and   you   came   to   visit   me (Matthew 25:35-36).

After   making   this   extraordinary   statement,   he   deliberately emphasized how closely he identified with those in need:

> I tell you the truth, whatever you did for one of the least of these brothers of mine, you did for me (Matthew 25:40).

Living responsibly for Christ also requires that we engage in making disciples. To his followers Jesus gave the Great Commission:

> Go and make disciples of all nations, baptizing them in the name of the Father and of the Son and of the Holy Spirit, and teaching them to obey everything I have commanded you (Matthew 28:19-20).

One of the principle results of this eight-week course in Devotional Prayer is reformation of life. Intimacy with Christ brings about change and improvement, even transformation. However, the change is not instantaneous. It is cumulative. It takes time to replace bad habits with healthy ones even when we persevere in well doing. Anger, lust, and greed do not disappear overnight. We do not expect perfection in this life, but we do expect significant improvement. How do we gauge that improvement? By checking to see whether our lives are increasingly characterized by these three qualities:

1.   A heightened love for God,

2.   An increasingly loving regard for family and others, and

3.   A more steadfast fulfillment, for Christ's sake, of our family and vocational responsibilities as well as of our obligations to the poor and to those who desire to become new disciples or more faithful disciples of Jesus.

SEVEN PRAYER EXERCISES

The prayer exercises in Week 8 are as follows: *"Empty Tomb," "Emmaus Road," "Upper Room," "Thomas," "Appearance at the Sea of Galilee," "The Great Commission,"* and *"Sheep and Goats."* The two final prayer exercises, *"The Great Commission" and "Sheep and Goats,"* conclude this prayer program with our Lord's mandates to make Christian disciples and to serve the poor and disadvantaged. The "Response" recommendations are deliberately brief so that you can proceed on your own.

Day One: "Empty Tomb"

Objective: Intimate knowledge of Christ that I might be *with* him, become *like* him, and live *for* him.

Scripture: John 20:1-18.

First point: Early in the morning Mary of Magdala saw that the stone had been taken away; she informed the other disciple.

Second point: Peter and the other disciple ran to the empty tomb. They saw the strips of linen lying there, as well as the burial cloth that had been around Jesus' head. The cloth was folded up by itself, separate from the linen. The other disciple believed.

Third point: Jesus appeared to Mary and called her by name.

Your Response:

❖ Begin your prayer period with a triumphant Easter hymn: *"Christ the Lord Is Risen Today"* or one you prefer. Try to enter into the joy and celebration of the hymn. You may want to sing full voice or softly, at normal pace or slowly. Do whatever best enables you to enter into the meaning and emotion of the words and music.

❖ Use Preparatory Prayer to ask the Lord to grant you the grace to be glad and rejoice intensely because of the glory of Christ, our risen Lord.

❖   Using the Prayer of Imaginative Contemplation, visualize the Scripture passage with special attention to each of the three points listed above. Come alive to the sights, smells, sounds, tastes, and feelings of the event.

　　　As you imagine this scene, step into the story so that you can be among those who first saw the empty tomb. Hear the Lord say the name "Mary!" Invite him also to say your name in a way that you can hear it.

　　　Seek to find one Attachment Insight (A) that you can grasp profoundly. Where does spiritual delight seem to be greatest?

❖   Enter into the Prayer of Adoration by praising Christ for who he is and for what his resurrection has accomplished.

❖   Sit humbly and gratefully in the presence of the Lord in the Prayer of Rest for several minutes. After a time, move away from the images of the story to a sense of oneness with Christ. He is the living, resurrected Lord and dwells in your heart. Rejoice and rest in that reality. As your mind wanders, bring your thoughts back by returning to your insight. Then return to quiet communion with the risen Lord.

Day Two: "Emmaus Road"

Objective:　Intimate knowledge of Christ that I might be *with* him, become *like* him, and live *for* him.

Scripture:　Luke 24:13-35.

First point:　He appears to the disciples on the Emmaus road.

Second point:　He reprimands them, explaining to them what was said in all the Scriptures concerning himself

Third point:　He remains with them, breaks bread and gives it to them. They recognize him in the breaking of the bread. Then he disappears. They return to the disciples in Jerusalem and tell them how Jesus was known to them in the breaking of the bread.

Your Response:

✛   After singing an Easter hymn or several Easter hymns, use Preparatory Prayer to ask the Lord for the grace to exult over the glory of Christ, our risen Lord, and over the two great means of spiritual illumination: the Christ-centered exposition of Scripture and the Breaking of Bread.

✛   Use Meditative Reading as you pray through Luke 24:13-35. Read the paragraphs several times. Sense the significance of the text when it states: "beginning with Moses and *all* the Prophets, he explained to them what was said in *all* the Scriptures concerning himself" (Luke 23:27, italics added).

   Reread those words or phrases that comfort, disturb, convict, or invigorate you. As you meditate on those words or phrases, think about them, weigh them, ponder them, and apply them to your daily activities. Then ask what type of Insight they represent: Principle (P), Attachment (A), Interior (I), or Detachment (D).

   Be conscious of any consolations that you may feel during the prayer exercise and give thanks to God for them.

✛   Assuming that you have been led to an insight that has given you intimate knowledge of Christ and that you consequently feel a deep love for him and a desire to serve him, praise and adore him in the Prayer of Adoration. Then sit humbly and gratefully in the presence of the victorious and resurrected Lord.

Day Three: *"Jesus Appears to His Disciples"*

<u>Objective</u>:   Intimate knowledge of Christ that I might be *with* him, become *like* him, and live *for* him.

<u>Scripture</u>: John 20:19-23.

<u>First point</u>: The disciples were together in one place "for fear of the Jews."

<u>Second point</u>: Jesus came and stood right in the middle of them and said, "Peace be with you! As the Father has sent me, I am sending you."

Third point: He breathed on them the Holy Spirit, saying, "Receive the Holy Spirit. If you forgive anyone his sins, they are forgiven; if you do not forgive them, they are not forgiven."

Your Response:

After singing a hymn and offering a Preparatory Prayer, use the Prayer of Consideration predominantly during this prayer exercise. At certain points, you may want to try mixing in Meditative Reading and Imaginative Contemplation. Intentionally look for the four types of insights: Principle, Attachment, Interior, Detachment (PAID). Seek an Attachment Insight (A) that draws you to the risen Lord. Express devotion to the Lord in the Prayer of Adoration and then relax in the Lord for several minutes, using the Prayer of Rest. Conclude by asking the Holy Spirit to fill you. Receive the peace of the risen Christ and rest in him.

Day Four: "Thomas"

Objective: Intimate knowledge of Christ that I might be *with* him, become *like* him, and live *for* him.

Scripture: John 20:24-29.

First point: Thomas would not believe.

Second point: One week later, Jesus appeared to Thomas.

Third point: Thomas believed saying, "My Lord and my God!" Christ said, "Because you have seen me, you have believed; blessed are those who have not seen and yet have believed."

Your Response:

Use your own initiative, with the Holy Spirit alongside as your teacher and guide. Consider concluding this meditation with a deep offering of yourself to Christ using the words of Thomas as you address Jesus as "My Lord and my God!"

Day Five: *"Appearance at the Sea of Galilee"*

Objective: Intimate knowledge of Christ that I might be *with* him, become *like* him, and live *for* him.

Scripture: John 21:1-17.

First point: Jesus appeared to seven of his disciples who were fishing. They had fished all night and had caught nothing. By casting the net at his command "they were unable to haul the net in because of the large number of fish."

Second point: Through this miracle John recognized him, and said to Peter, "It is the Lord!" Peter jumped into the water and came to Christ.

Third point: Jesus gave them bread and fish to eat. After he had tested the love of Peter three times, Jesus instructed Peter to "Feed my sheep."

Your Response:

Seek the direction of the Holy Spirit all the way. Ask him to help you rejoice intensely in the glory of Christ our resurrected Lord.

Day Six: *"The Great Commission"*

Objective: Intimate knowledge of Christ that I might be *with* him, become *like* him, and live *for* him.

Scripture: Matthew 28:16-20.

First point: The disciples, at the command of Christ, went to Galilee, to the mountain where Jesus had told them to go, where they worshiped him.

Second point: Christ then said to them: "All authority in heaven and on earth has been given to me."

Third point: He sent them throughout the whole world to make disciples saying, "Therefore go and make disciples of all nations, baptizing them in the name of the Father and of the Son and of the Holy Spirit, and teaching them to obey everything I have commanded you. And surely I will be with you always, to the very end of the age" (Matthew 28:19-20).

Your Response:

Seek direction from the Holy Spirit, your Spiritual Director.

Day Seven: "Sheep and Goats"

Objective: Intimate knowledge of Christ that I might be *with* him, become *like* him, and live *for* him.

Scripture: Matthew 25:31-46.

First point: The Son of Man comes in his glory, and as King and Judge, separates the sheep from the goats.

Second point: The evidence that the Judge and King produces.

Third point: Intimacy with Christ through service.

Fourth point: The future of the righteous and the unrighteous.

Your Response:

The Holy Spirit is your Spiritual Director. Seek his guidance.

FRIENDS ON THE JOURNEY

Bob — The presence of God in daily living

Bob said that the final prayer exercise on the "Sheep and Goats" challenged him to practice the presence of God by serving Jesus through serving those less fortunate than himself. He felt this was how Matthew 25 was meant to be understood and asked whether this could be one way to have a "*with* Christ" experience apart from his prayer time.

I was delighted to hear Bob's question. I had included the sober passage on the "Sheep and Goats," Matthew 25:31-46, with the hope that the correlation would be apparent between being *with* Christ in prayer and being *with* Christ in the service of the "least of these my brothers."

As I shared with Bob, I referred to Mother Teresa, perhaps the most striking example of one who saw Christ in others. The motivation that sustained her and continues to sustain her Missionaries of Charity is the teaching of Matthew 25.

For instance, when Mother Teresa was asked whether she found it easy to carry out her work, she answered:

> We are taught from the very first moment to discover Christ under the distressing disguise of the poor, the sick, the outcasts. Christ presents himself to us under every disguise: the dying, the paralytic, the leper, the invalid, the orphan. It is faith that makes our work, which demands both special preparation and a special calling, easy or at least more bearable. Without faith, our work could become an obstacle for our religious life since we come across blasphemy, wickedness, and atheism at every turn.[4]

There, in capsule form, is the secret of her success. The leprosy patient whose wounds crawled with maggots was not a repulsive person. He was Jesus in a "distressing disguise." And as she knelt next to him and cleaned his wounds, she talked tenderly to him in his native tongue as though she were talking to Jesus, for, according to his words, she was.

Matthew 25, as I understand it, urges us to discover Jesus in every relationship, especially in those who are in need. In this eight-week prayer program, we have learned how we can experience communion with Christ in prayer. In Matthew 25, Christ shows us how we have an expanded opportunity to experience communion *with* him in service:

> For *I* was hungry and you gave *me* something to eat, *I* was thirsty and you gave *me* something to drink, *I* was a stranger and you invited *me* in, *I* needed clothes and you clothed *me*, *I* was sick and you looked after *me*, *I* was in prison and you came to visit *me* (Matthew 25:35-36, italics added).

This emphasis on service was very much in line with the spirituality of Ignatius. Knowing Bob would be interested, I mentioned that Ignatius, as General of the Society of Jesus, fought against the tendency among some of the Jesuits to spend hours in prayer at the expense of serving.[5]

Cathy — A good plan for future prayer

Cathy was positive as she concluded the prayer program. The prayer exercises had enabled her to receive insights into the person and character of Christ that had drawn her to greater love for him.

Consolations had filled her eyes with tears and her lips with praise. She had experienced a depth of communion with the Lord that was completely new to her. She had worked through the anxiety involved in losing her position, and had stuck with the prayer program despite the temptation on a number of occasions to quit. In addition to the subjective changes, the prayer experience inspired her to a new level of caring for others, and of sharing with others her experience of closeness to Christ.

Toward the end of our time of interaction, she said: "My plan is to go back through the eight-week program one more time, and to do it with two friends. What do you think?"

I told her that I thought it was a good idea, and that I was very pleased that she felt motivated to do so. Intimacy with Christ was her continuing privilege and joy, and she would be able to help her friends by explaining to them the skills and principles she had learned. We prayed together, asking the Lord to continue deepening our love for him, and then we offered ourselves to God using the prayer of Ignatius with which he concludes the *Spiritual Exercises.*

> Take, Lord, and receive all my liberty, my memory, my understanding, and my entire will — all that I have and call my own. You have given it all to me. To you, Lord, I return it. Everything is yours; do with it what you will. Give me only your love and your grace. That is enough for me.[6]

APPENDIX

USING THIS BOOK WITH OTHERS

This prayer program may be scheduled as a weekly meeting for eight weeks at any time of the year. However, the best time of the year to use this book with individuals or small groups is from Lent through the first week of Eastertide. The prayer program could begin on the week of Ash Wednesday, continuing week by week through Lent. Week 7, which deals with the events of Holy Thursday and Good Friday, would coincide with Holy Week from Palm Sunday to Holy Saturday. Week 8, which deals with the resurrection of Christ and his resurrection appearances, would coincide with Easter Sunday and the first week of Eastertide.

Training in Devotional Prayer can take place on an individual basis or in groups numbering from two to several hundred. Here are some recommendations for group use.

1. A Mentor Guiding a Student of Prayer

A pastor or someone mature in the faith who has gone through the material in this book can use this training program as a mentoring tool. The material has been written so that it can be used without a personal guide; nevertheless, a mentor can provide a beneficial service by meeting with someone on a weekly basis. The mentor can answer questions, rejoice with the individual over the insights received and consolations experienced, reinforce the instructions, encourage every evidence of progress, hold the student accountable to a faithful fulfillment of the program, and pray with and for the student. This can be a rewarding process of inner transformation for both mentor and student.

2. Group of Two or Three Individuals

Two or three individuals could agree to meet on a weekly basis, provide feedback to one another, hold one another accountable, and pray for one another. The weekly meeting would be a debrief/mutual support/prayer session.

Five or six of the following points could provide a simple format for an *Interaction Plan.*

(1) Pray for the presence and guidance of the Lord.

(2) Ask one another if there are questions or comments regarding the written instructions at the beginning of each chapter.

(3) Take turns giving feedback on the prayer exercises covered during the week. Involve as many participants as possible, with each person reporting on at least one exercise.

(4) Indicate to one another which Mental Prayer was used and the main insight gained from the exercise.

(5) Invite participants to comment on any experience of Heart Prayer. Ask how they handled it.

(6) Ask whether there was a special Prayer of Petition inspired by the prayer period and whether further prayer support is desired.

(7) Ask whether the Prayer of Adoration was entered into and what the substance of that prayer was.

(8) Inquire how the Prayer of Rest was managed.

(9) Ask what proved to be helpful or distracting.

(10) Ask whether the session concluded with a prayer of self-offering in service for the Lord.

(11) Ask how Devotional Prayer is affecting relationships at home and at work.

(12) Pray together to thank the Lord for his presence and guidance and to ask God's blessing on one another.

Another **Interaction Plan** approach would be to use the Prayer Response Sheet (p. 67) as a feedback interaction guide. The Response Sheet lists the items in Devotional Prayer and can be used for feedback in a number of ways. The easiest approach would be to invite each participant, when giving feedback on a specific prayer exercise, to select one item or more from the Response Sheet and to comment on how that item was helpful in handling the prayer exercise.

3. Small Group of Five to Eight

The pastor or someone with spiritual maturity and insight should lead the group of five to eight. It would be essential for the leader to have a thorough grasp of the teachings and skills of this program so that he or she could emphasize important principles, respond to the questions of group participants, and work with participants on prayer skills. The group would meet for encouragement, accountability, questions/answers, the sharing of insights and blessings, direction, and support.

An advantage of a group approach is that individuals can instruct and inspire one another as they share insights. Someone, for instance, could comment on the generosity of Jesus when he provided a great quantity of wine, and of the very best quality; or how flexible and gentle Jesus was in going along with his mother's wish. Another could agree, but might suggest that Jesus, since he always did what pleased the Father (John 8:29), must have sought inward confirmation from the Father and been given consent to respond favorably to his mother's request. As others add to the list of admirable qualities, the meeting can become an inspiring worship experience as individuals take turns describing the attributes of the Lord.

It would be especially important to encourage the participants to share their experience with Heart Prayer and the Prayer of Rest since they might be reluctant to talk about these matters in a group setting. The leader would need a good understanding of the forms of prayer described in Weeks 2 and 4. The pastor or lay leader facilitating such a group could use the *Interaction Plan* suggested in item number two above.

4. **A Seminar or Weekend Retreat on Devotional Prayer for a Sunday School Class, Men's or Women's Group, Small Group, or Congregation**

Segments of the book could be used at a weekend or Saturday retreat or conference to teach various aspects of Devotional Prayer such as principles of spiritual direction, Meditative Reading, Imaginative Contemplation, the Prayer of Consideration, Heart Prayer, the Prayer of Adoration, the Prayer of Rest, Attachment Insights (A), and the other types of insights. The seminar or retreat would have to be conducted by a seasoned leader thoroughly familiar with the principles, skills, and modes of prayer taught in this book. Personally going through the eight-week prayer guide several times, mentoring a student of prayer one-on-one, leading a group of two or three individuals or a small group through the eight-week process — all of this would be essential preparation for leading a retreat or seminar on Devotional Prayer.

After the seminar or retreat, conferees could be encouraged to go through the prayer program on their own or with another individual or a small group as suggested in points two or three above. Ideas on what could be included in a seminar or a retreat consisting of two, three, or four sessions are included in the following paragraphs.

Two-Session Retreat or Seminar

You could begin by talking about the need for maintaining and nurturing an intimate relationship with Christ. My story as I describe it in the Preface or perhaps an illustration from the personal experience of the retreat leader or one of the retreat participants could be used.

You could then follow with a discussion of the *"With Christ, Like Christ, For Christ"* progression or the importance of focusing on God rather than focusing on self. I deal with both of these subjects in the Introduction.

Third, you could teach the first five principles dealt with in Week 1: (a) Understand that God welcomes you to prayer just as you are; (b) Recognize that the Holy Spirit is your Spiritual Director; (c) Seek to be flexible; (d) Learn to be guided through peace or turbulence; (e) Seek intimate understanding of the truth.

All of the three points mentioned above could be briefly done in a half-hour. The points would be repeated and reinforced during the feedback sessions.

Next would be the opportunity to pray for half an hour over the prayer exercise "Most Appealing" (p. 49). Distribute the prayer exercise, go over it, and answer any questions. Ask the participants to find a quiet and, if possible, private place and invite them to return after a half-hour to forty-five-minute prayer period.

Feedback questions could include: "What was your most appealing scene or episode?" This becomes a lovely worship experience as participants share the many ways in which Jesus is wonderful. Also ask: "Did you experience Heart Prayer?" "Did you thank the Lord for it?" "Were you able to move into the Prayer of Adoration?" "Were you able to quiet yourself and experience the Prayer of Rest?" Briefly explain these terms. The feedback will provide opportunity for additional instruction and encouragement.

For the second prayer period, use the Prayer Exercise, *"Baptism"* (p. 68). Prepare the people by discussing Imaginative Contemplation as described and explained in the materials provided in Week 2. Go over the objective of the exercise and the process material ("Your Response"), and answer any questions so that the prayer assignment is clear to everyone. Encourage the people to look for Attachment Insights, explaining the term (see p. 60) and offering a few reasons as to why these will facilitate greater devotion to Jesus. Release the people for a half-hour of private devotional prayer.

The feedback session provides an opportunity for the people to share their insights or their experience with Imaginative Contemplation, Heart Prayer, Prayer of Adoration, and Prayer of Rest. They can also ask questions or express concerns they might have. I have found this session to be filled with energy. People are eager to share the insights God has given them. Some may be willing to talk about their experience of joy as they imaginatively viewed (many of them for the first time) various aspects of the Lord's baptism.

Three-Session Retreat or Seminar

Begin the first of three sessions with "Most Appealing." Then, for the second session, introduce Meditative Reading as described and explained in Week 2. Ask the group to meditate on the Prayer Exercise *"Lazarus"* (p. 128). Go over the objective of the exercise and the "Your Response" material, answering questions so that the prayer assignment is clear. Encourage the people to look for Attachment Insights (A), explaining the term and reminding them why these increase devotion to Jesus. Release the people for a half-hour or forty-five minutes of private devotional prayer.

In the feedback session, provide opportunity for participants to share their insights and experiences with Meditative Reading, Heart Prayer, Prayer of Adoration, and Prayer of Rest. Reinforce the spiritual principles and other introductory materials taught in the opening session. Follow this second session with a third on Imaginative Contemplation similar to that described in the *Two Sessions Retreat or Seminar* material above.

The reason I place an exercise using Meditative Reading before Imaginative Contemplation is because the participants may be less likely to appreciate fully the value of Meditative Reading if it is introduced in the third rather than the second session of the retreat. Meditative Reading is generally less sensational than Imaginative Contemplation and takes greater sensitivity. If Imaginative Contemplation is used with a group unfamiliar with it before an exercise in Meditative Reading, the dramatic use of the imagination in Imaginative Contemplation tends to overshadow Meditative Reading.

Four-Session Retreat or Seminar

In the fourth session, the Prayer of Consideration explained in Week 2 and the four types of insights described in Week 3 can be introduced. The participants would have been urged to seek Attachment Insights (A) in each of the previous sessions. The other three kinds of insights — Principle Insights (P), Interior Insights (I), and Detachment Insights (D) — can be introduced with an explanation of their value. The Prayer Exercise *"Peter's Confession of Christ"* (p. 112) could be assigned, with participants using the Prayer of Consideration to come up with each of the four types of insights.

During the feedback session, ask for examples of each of the four types of insights. There are usually requests for clarification on the classification of insights. Provide opportunity for retreat participants to express how the Lord made himself known to them during their prayer period. Also invite them to comment on their experience of intimacy or communion with the Lord. Affirm the prayer experience of participants and assure them that the Spirit desires to lead them into a deeper relationship with God through Devotional Prayer.

NOTES

Preface

1. Alexander B. Aronis, "Spiritual Direction: A Project Modeled on St. Ignatius' Spiritual Exercises," Doctor of Ministry Dissertation, Fuller Theological Seminary, Pasadena California, 1981.

2. Susan Wise Bauer, "The Myth of a Better Prayer Life," *Christianity Today*, 27 Apr. 1998: 28.

3. Ibid., 31.

Introduction: Preparing for the Journey

1. H. Richard Niebuhr, quoted in Philip Yancey, *What's So Amazing About Grace?* (Grand Rapids, Michigan: Zondervan Publishing House, 1997), 13-14.

2. Billy Graham, *Just as I Am: The Autobiography of Billy Graham* (San Francisco: HarperSanFrancisco Zondervan, 1997), 724.

3. Wendy Murray Zoba, "Bright to the End," *Christianity Today*, 1 Oct. 2001: 59.

4. John Stott, *Life in Christ* (Grand Rapids: Baker Books, 1996), 108.

5. Ibid., 109.

6. Charles R. Swindoll, *Intimacy with the Almighty: Encountering Christ in the Secret Places of Your Life* (Dallas: Word, 1996), 9.

7. Ibid., 9-10.

8. Ignatius of Loyola was the youngest child of a noble Spanish family. He was engaged in battle in 1521 when a French cannonball shattered his leg. During a long convalescence, he found himself drawn to spiritual reading.

He had a dream of "converting the infidel" and took steps to acquire an education to be able to "help souls." He spoke to people about "spiritual things," even when the Inquisition could imprison anyone who conversed with others about personal religion without having a theological degree or priestly ordination. Ignatius was in fact imprisoned in several cities by order of the Inquisition.

He left Spain and continued his education at the University of Paris. When he completed his Master of Arts degree, he organized a series of methods or activities for opening oneself to God's Spirit. These exercises became a handbook for the guide who would coach persons engaged in "making the Exercises." The handbook was completed in 1541 and in time came to be called *The Spiritual Exercises of St. Ignatius.*

In 1540, Ignatius founded the Society of Jesus. Today the Society numbers about 23,000 priests and brothers spread out in almost every country in the world. Members of the Society of Jesus are called Jesuits. See George W. Traub, S.J., *Do You Speak Ignatian? A Glossary of Terms Used in Ignatian and Jesuit Circles* (Cincinnati: Xavier University, 1997), 3, 6-7.

9. Ignatius, *The Spiritual Exercises of St. Ignatius: Based on Studies in the Language of the Autograph,* trans. by Louis J. Puhl, S.J. (Chicago: Loyola University Press, 1951), 54-55, paragraphs 122-126. Ignatius refers to this as "Applying the Five Senses." The paragraph numbers have become the standard mode of reference for the *Spiritual Exercises.* Most translations of the *Exercises* use the same paragraph numbers. I will provide a page number and a paragraph number as follows: 54-55, #122-126.

10. *The Spiritual Exercises of St. Ignatius* has an extraordinary publishing history. "According to one plausible estimate worked out in 1948, by then the *Exercises* had been published, either alone or with commentaries, some 4,500 times — an average of once a month for four centuries — and the number of copies printed was around 4,500,000. Around the world today the *Exercises* are being made by greater numbers than ever before." See *The Spiritual Exercises of Saint Ignatius* a Translation and Commentary by George E. Ganss, S.J. (St. Louis: The Institute of Jesuit Sources, 1992), 8.

11. Dallas Willard, *The Divine Conspiracy: Rediscovering Our Hidden Life in God* (San Francisco: HarperSanFrancisco, A Division of HarperCollins Publishers, 1998), 370.

12. Philip Yancey, *The Jesus I Never Knew* (Grand Rapids: Zondervan Publishing House, 1995), 269.

13. Ibid.

PART I: SEEING YOURSELF AS GOD SEES YOU

Week 1: Working with Spiritual Direction

1. Martin Luther, *Luther's Works,* Vol. 21, ed. Helmut T. Loehmann, "Sermon on the Mount" (Philadelphia: Muhlenberg Press, 1960), 141.

2. John Chrysostom, *A Select Library of the Nicene and Post-Nicene Fathers,* Vol. 10, ed. Philip Schaff, "The Works of St. Chrysostom, The Gospel of St. Matthew" (New York: The Christian Literature Company, 1888), 134.

3. Karl Rahner, *Ignatius of Loyola* (London: Collins, 1979), 13.

4. Ignatius, op. cit., 1-2, #2.

5. Ibid, 2, #2.

6. John H. English, *Spiritual Freedom* (Ontario: Loyola House, 1979), 13.

7. Dietrich Bonhoeffer, *Life Together* (New York: Harper & Brothers Publishers, 1954), 82.

8. Luther, op. cit., 139.

9. Richard J. Foster, *Prayer: Finding the Heart's True Home* (San Francisco: Harper Collins Publishers, 1992), 74.

10. C. S. Lewis, *Letter to Malcolm: Chiefly on Prayer* (New York: A Harvest/HBCS Book, 1964), 18.

11. Ignatius, op. cit., 36, #76.

12. Thomas H. Green, S.J., *A Vacation with the Lord: a Personal, Directed Retreat with Thomas H. Green, S.J.* (Notre Dame, Indiana: Ave Maria Press, 1986), 24.

PART II: THE LIFE AND MINISTRY OF CHRIST

Week 2: Praying in Various Ways

1. Ignatius, op. cit., for "Preparatory Prayer" 25, #46; for "Meditative Reading" 110, #252 and #254; for "Imaginative Contemplation" 25, #47, 109, #248; for "Prayer of Consideration" 26, #48, 101-103, #234-237; for "Heart Prayer" 142, #316, 25, #48; for "Prayer of Petition" 101, #233, 111, #257; for "Prayer of Adoration" 102, #234, 110, #252; for "Prayer of Rest" 110, #254, 112, #258.

2. Ibid., 110-111, #249-257. Ignatius called Meditative Reading the "Second Method of Prayer" and used it in contemplating the meaning of each word of a prayer such as the "Our Father."

3. Ibid., 54-55, #121-126.

4. John A. MacKay, quoted in Paul Yonggi Cho, *The Holy Spirit, My Senior Partner: Understanding the Holy Spirit and His Gifts* (Altamonte Springs, Florida: Creation House, 1989), 20-21.

5. Ignatius, op. cit., 142, #316.

6. Martin Luther, *The Large Catechism of Martin Luther,* trans. Robert H. Fisher (Philadelphia: Fortress Press, 1959), 89.

7. John Calvin, *Institutes of the Christian Religion,* ed. John T. McNeill, Vol. 2 (Philadelphia: The Westminster Press, 1960), 853.

8. Foster, op. cit., 179.

9. Calvin, op. cit., 852.

10. John McAnulty, quoted in Aronis, op. cit., 77. John McAnulty is the Director of the House of Prayer for Priests in Los Angeles, California.

11. Ignatius, op. cit., 110, #254.

12. "Most Appealing" is my adaptation of Ignatius' thematic exercise "Kingdom of Christ," ibid., 43-45, #91-99. I am indebted to John McAnulty, S.J., for this adaptation.

Week 3: Delighting in the Lord
1. Ignatius, op. cit., 1, #1.
2. Willard, op. cit., 273.
3. A. W. Tozer, *The Pursuit of God* (Harrisburg: Christian Publications, Inc., 1948), 90-91.
4. Calvin, op. cit., 854.
5. Karl Barth, *Church Dogmatics* (Edinburgh: T. & T. Clark, 1957) Vol. II, Part 1, 403.
6. "Two Banners" is my adaptation of Ignatius' thematic exercise "A Meditation on Two Standards," Ignatius, op. cit., 60-63, #136-148.
7. Ibid., 2, #2.
8. Frederick Dale Bruner, *The Christbook: A Historical/Theological Commentary Matthew 1-12* (Waco, Texas: Word Books Publishers, 1987), 186.
9. Chrysostom, op. cit., Vol. 10, 117.

Week 4: Resting in Jesus
1. James Stewart, *A Man in Christ: The Vital Elements of St. Paul's Religion* (New York and London: Harper and Brothers Publishers, *n.d.*), 147.
2. Ibid., 11-12.
3. M. Basil Pennington, *Centering Prayer: Renewing an Ancient Christian Prayer Form* (Garden City, New York: Doubleday & Company, Inc., 1980), 107-108.
4. Thomas Keating, *Open Mind, Open Heart: The Contemplative Dimension of the Gospel* (New York: The Continuum Publishing Company, 1997), 53-67. See also Thomas Keating, *The Method of Centering Prayer* (Butler, New Jersey: Contemplative Outreach, LTD., 1995), 6.
5. Ibid., 91.
6. Kallistos Ware, "The Origins of the Jesus Prayer: Diadochus, Gaza, Sinai," *The Study of Spirituality*. eds. Cheslyn Jones, Geoffrey Wainwright, Edward Yarnold, S.J. (New York: Oxford University Press, 1986), 176-178.
7. Kallistos Ware, *The Power of the Name: The Jesus Prayer in Orthodox Spirituality* (Fairacres, Oxford: SLG Press Convent of the Incarnation, 1986), 5.
8. Ware, *The Study of Spirituality*, op. cit., 184.
9. Lev Gillet, *The Jesus Prayer* (Crestwood, New York 10707: St. Vladimir's Seminary Press, 1987), 93.

10. Ware, *The Power of The Name,* op. cit., 13.

11. Climacus and the other Eastern Fathers cited by Ware, *The Study of Spirituality*, op. cit., 181-183.

12. Ignatius, op. cit., 112, #258-260.

13. *Pilgrim: The Way of a Pilgrim and The Pilgrim Continues His Way,* trans. Helen Bacovcin (New York: Doubleday, 1992), 41.

14. Sergei Hackel, "The Eastern Tradition from the Tenth to the Twentieth Century: Russian," *The Study of Spirituality*, op. cit., 272.

15. "Three Types of Persons" is my adaptation of Ignatius' thematic exercise "Three Classes of Men," Ignatius, op. cit., 64-65, #149-157.

Week 5: Dealing with Desolation

1. Ignatius, op. cit., 142, #317.

2. Thomas H. Green, S.J., *Drinking from a Dry Well* (Notre Dame, Indiana: Ave Maria Press, 1991), 23.

3. David L. Fleming, S.J., *The Spiritual Exercises of Saint Ignatius: A Literal Translation and A Contemporary Reading* (Saint Louis: The Institute of Jesuit Sources, 1978), 211, #322.

4. Bonhoeffer, *Life Together*, op. cit., 82.

Week 6: Finding God's Will for You

1. Ignatius, op. cit., 74, #175-177.

2. Ibid., 148, #333.

3. Ibid., 147, #330.

4. Green, *A Vacation with the Lord,* op. cit., 124-125.

5. From the Westminster Shorter Catechism of 1647, one of the most widely used Protestant catechisms of the past few centuries. It begins by asking: "What is the chief end of man?" The answer: "Man's chief end is to glorify God, and to enjoy him forever." See Philip Schaff, *The Creeds of Christendom, with a History and Critical Notes,* vol. III (New York: Harper & Brothers, Franklin Square, 1919), 676.

6. "Four Degrees of Humility" is my adaptation of Ignatius' thematic exercise "Three Kinds of Humility," Ignatius, op. cit., 69-70, #165-168.

7. Green, *A Vacation with the Lord,* op. cit., 148.

PART III: THE SUFFERING OF CHRIST

Week 7: Eating According to Spiritual Perspectives

1. Dallas Willard, *The Spirit of the Disciplines: Understanding How God Changes Lives* (San Francisco: Harper & Row, Publishers, 1988), 166.

2. Ignatius, op. cit., 11, #21.

3. Richard Foster, *Celebration of Discipline: The Path to Spiritual Growth,* rev. ed. (New York: Harper & Row, Publishers, 1988), 56.

4. Tito Colliander, *Way of the Ascetics: The Ancient Tradition of Discipline and Inner Growth,* trans. Katherine Ferre, intro, Kenneth Leech (New York: St. Vladimir's Seminary Press, 1985), p.75.

5. Calvin, op. cit., 1241-1242.

6. Martin Luther, *What Luther Says,* vol. 1 (St. Louis: Concordia Publishing House, 1959), 506.

7. Dietrich Bonhoeffer, *The Cost of Discipleship* (New York: The Macmillan Company, 1948), 146.

8. Ibid., 146.

9. Cornelius Plantinga, Jr., "First Prayer," *The Reformed Journal* 38 (Nov. 1988): 3.

10. à Kempis, op. cit., 40.

11. Ignatius, op. cit., 89-91, #210-217.

12. Neal Barnard, M.D., *Food for Life: How the New Four Food Groups Can Save Your Life* (New York: Harmony Books, 1993), 142-161.

13. Sara Hammel, "Mamma mia! No Meatballs?" *U. S. News & World Report,* 1 March 1999: 65.

14. John Wesley, "Sermon XXVII, On Our Lord's Sermon on the Mount," *The Works of John Wesley,* vol. 5 (Albany: Sage Software, 1995), 441.

15. William Law, *A Serious Call to a Devout and Holy Life* (Grand Rapids: Wm. B. Erdmans Publishing Co., 1966, orig. 1728), 112.

16. Bill Bright, *Seven Basic Steps to Successful Fasting and Prayer* (Orlando: New Life Publication, 1995), 6.

17. Ignatius, op. cit., 84, #203.

PART IV: THE RESURRECTION OF CHRIST
Week 8: Charting Your Prayer Future

1. Allister E. McGrath, "The Biography of God: Narrative Theologians Point to the Divine Stories that Shape Our Lives," *Christianity Today* (22 July 1991), 22-24.

2. E. W. Trueman Dicken, "Teresa of Jesus and John of the Cross," *Study of Spirituality,* op. cit., 364.

3. Ignatius, op. cit., 78, #189.

4. Mother Teresa, *Loving Jesus,* ed. Jose Luis Gonzalez-Balado (Ann Arbor: Servant Publication, 1991), 126.

5. William A. Barry, S.J., *Finding God in All things: A Companion to the Spiritual Exercises of St. Ignatius* (Notre Dame: Ave Maria Press, 1991), 108.

6. Fleming, op. cit., 141, #234.

About the Author

Alex Aronis was raised in Los Angeles and lives with his wife, Carol, in Cincinnati, Ohio. For 16 years he served as a Navy Chaplain, and for 19 years he served as pastor of the Union Church of Manila and Kenwood Baptist Church in Cincinnati, Ohio. He is currently the Senior Pastor of the Union Church of Manila.

He graduated from the U. S. Naval Academy, Fuller Theological Seminary, the University of Southern California, and has a Ph. D. from The American University.

Alex Aronis conducts retreats, workshops, and seminars for churches, schools, and missionary organizations. For further information contact Alex at his email address alexaronis@unionchurch.ph and/or log on to the website of Union Church of Manila <www.unionchurch.ph>.

Printed in the United States
132456LV00003B/6/A